TEXAS

It's Like A Whole Other Count

**GREAT FLAVORS OF TEXAS is
dedicated to the wonderful and diverse
people of Texas who have created the Texas
cooking experience! Texans are passionate about
Texas and passion permeates their culinary wizardry. Texas cooking is
its people, and this variety produces flavors that not only Texans but
enjoy magnificent and distinctive food can become passionate about!**

1

SOUTHERN FLAVORS PUBLICATIONS

P.O. Box 922
Pine Bluff, Arkansas 71613

Please use the order form in the back of the book to order additional copies of
GREAT FLAVORS OF TEXAS, and other cookbooks in the Great Flavors series!

WATCH FOR NEW PUBLICATIONS FROM SOUTHERN FLAVORS, INC.
ISBN 0-9618137-2-5
USA

Printed by
Favorite Recipes® Press • P.O. Box 305142 • Nashville, Tennessee 37230
1-800-358-0560

For Sherry and Jan — It's finally done!!

FOREWORD

Texas <u>is</u> a whole other country! It covers 267,339 square miles and is second only to Alaska in size. While working on GREAT FLAVORS OF TEXAS, we learned that the number of outstanding cooks in the Lone Star State is equal to or exceeds its square miles!! Thus, GREAT FLAVORS OF TEXAS grew from a projected cookbook of 160 pages and 250 plus recipes to its present size of 192 pages and 387 (kitchen-tested) recipes!!

We give a Texas-sized thanks to the Tourism Division of the State's Department of Commerce, the Office of the Governor, and the Department of Agriculture for the invaluable assistance in providing material for the Texas Facts, Festivals, Notables, Places, Treasures, and Texas "Big" that are sprinkled throughout the book. Special thanks go to John Crawford of COLLIN STREET BAKERY in Corsicana, Nacy Beckham of BRAZO'S CAFE in Dallas, David Wallace of the TYLER SQUARE ANTIQUE MALL TEAROOM, Randy Barnett of DARYL'S BY DESIGN in Dallas, Bob LaRoche of CALICO COUNTY RESTAURANT in Amarillo, Renie Steves of CUISINE CONCEPTS in Fort Worth, David Lewis of JOHN HENRY'S RESTAURANT in Wimberley, Chef Michel Platz of the ANATOLE HOTEL in Dallas, MAMA'S HOFBRAU RESTAURANT in San Antonio, Susan and Marc Hall of the CISCO GRILL in Dallas, Chef Kevin Garvin of the ADOLPHUS HOTEL in Dallas, Chef William Ardid of CHEZ ARDID RESTAURANT in San Antonio, and Chef Steve Valenti of PATRIZIO'S RESTAURANT in Dallas.

Our hearty thanks also go to Governor Ann W. Richards, Mrs. Lyndon Baines Johnson, former Governor William P. Clements, Jr., Susan Teeple Aulur of FALL CREEK VINEYARDS, Virginia Sides of SIDES PEA FARM in Canton, Mike Hughes of BROKEN ARROW RANCH in Ingram, Anne Lindsey Greer, author of CUISINE OF THE AMERICAN SOUTHWEST, R.J.'S RESTAURANT in Uvalde, and FRANK LEWIS' ALAMO FRUIT COMPANY. Lastly, our very special thanks go to the Junior Leagues of Austin (NECESSITIES AND TEMPTATIONS COOKBOOK), Corpus Christi (FIESTA COOKBOOK), Galveston County (RARE COLLECTION COOKBOOK), Odessa (THE WILD WILD WEST COOKBOOK), San Antonio (FLAVORS COOKBOOK), and Waco (HEARTS AND FLOURS COOKBOOK).

GREAT FLAVORS OF TEXAS is a celebration of the distinctiveness and diversity of the Texas cooking experience. We hope that you enjoy using our cookbook as much as we have enjoyed developing and producing it! GREAT FLAVORS provides very definite flavors of Texas to the non-native and is a marvelous memento for the Texas native and visitor of the wonderful times and grand food that Texas offers!! We invite you to savor and enjoy!!!

Sherry Ferguson, Co-editor	**Jan Bennett Seger, Co-editor**	**Jeanne Verlenden &**
Dallas, Texas	**San Antonio, Texas**	**Dee Danaher, Editors**

TABLE OF
CONTENTS

APPETIZERS AND BEVERAGES

TEJAS GUACAMOLE DIP

3-4 medium avocados, peeled, pitted, & coarsely chopped
6-8 green onions & tops, pureed

2-3 garlic cloves, crushed
1/2 cup cottage cheese
1/2 cup mayonnaise
2 Tbsps. bottled Italian dressing

2 medium tomatoes, chopped
1 *jalapeno pepper, seeded & chopped

Combine well all ingredients; serve with favorite chips. The dip can be a super salad for six, served over shredded lettuce.
Yields about 3 cups.

Addie Baker Nold, Arlington, Texas

MRS. GRISSOM'S CHEESE JALAPENO DIP

1 lb. sharp Cheddar cheese, grated
1/2-1 (2 1/2 oz.) can *jalapenos, seeded & chopped

1 (16 oz.) jar mayonnaise
2 medium onions, finely chopped

2 cloves garlic, finely chopped
1/2 tsp. salt

Mix well all ingredients. Store in jars to enhance flavor; refrigerate. Serve with crackers or chips. Great for casual entertaining!
Yields 5-6 cups.

"This recipe is an original one created by my mother, Cleo Jones Grissom, of Carthage, Texas. It is my favorite!"

Coleen Grissom, San Antonio, Texas

*TEXAS FACT:
When handling hot Texas peppers such as jalapeno and serrano, cooks should use a bit of caution, wear rubber gloves, and be careful not to rub around eyes or face. When finished, cooks should wash their hands well!!

"BIG D" CHEESE 'N BEER DIP

1 (8 oz.) pkg. cream cheese
1/2 cup beer, cool but not cold
2-3 cloves garlic, crushed

1/4 cup beer, cool but not cold
8 ozs. sharp Cheddar cheese, diced

10-12 small whole sweet pickles, chopped
1 tsp. poppy seeds

In blender, mix cream cheese and half cup beer for 10 seconds; add next 3 ingredients; blend until smooth. Add remaining ingredients; blend for 5 seconds. Serve with tostados or chips. Men like this one!!

Makes 3 cups.

SOUTHWESTERN CORN DIP

2 (10 oz.) pkgs. frozen corn, cooked & drained
2 cups sharp Cheddar cheese, grated
1/4 tsp. Tabasco

1 (4 oz.) can diced pimentos, drained
1 1/2 Tbsps. jalapenos, chopped
2 Tbsps. cilantro, chopped

1 cup sour cream
1/2 cup mayonnaise
Salt to taste
Tortilla chips for dipping

In large bowl, combine all ingredients; cover; refrigerate. Serve with chips. That simple!

Yields approximately 7 sensational cups!

Sherry Ferguson, GREAT FLAVORS OF TEXAS

TEXAS NOTABLE:
Texas was home to Mildred "Babe" Didrikson Zaharias, who the Associated Press of Sportswriters voted to be the World's Greatest Athlete for the first half of the twentieth century. Babe, as she was affectionately called by all who knew her, was the best of her time in many sports including golf and tennis. She was named the Woman Athlete of the Year by the Associated Press six different years. No other athlete, either man or woman, has been awarded this honor that many times!

SCOREKEEPER'S ARTICHOKE DIP

1 (16 oz.) can artichoke
   hearts, drained
1/3 cup mayonnaise
6 ozs. cream cheese, softened

2 Tbsps. onion, chopped
Salt, pepper, & red pepper
   to taste
Juice of 1/2 lemon

4 slices bacon, fried crisp
   & chopped
Corn chips

In blender, chop artichokes to pulp; add next 2 ingredients; mix until smooth; add remaining ingredients; chill. Serve with chips.
Makes about 3 cups.

Jane McGilvray, McAllen, Texas

PICANTE DIP

2 small onions, finely chopped
3 Tbsps. salad oil
1 clove garlic, pressed
1 (6 oz.) can tomato paste

1 (1 lb. 13 oz.) can whole
   tomatoes
1/3 cup jalapenos, minced
1 tsp. sugar

Salt & pepper to taste
1/2 cup sharp Cheddar
   cheese, grated

Saute onions in oil until soft; add next 6 ingredients; mix well. Simmer for 2 hours; sprinkle with cheese. Serve warm with favorite chips!!
Makes one quart.

Patty Buescher, McAllen, Texas

TEXAS PECAN 'N CHEESE DIP

1 (8 oz.) pkg. cream cheese
1 (8 oz.) carton sour cream
1/2 - 1 cup pecans, chopped

1 (2 1/2 oz.) jar pimentos,
   chopped
10 stuffed green olives, chopped

Watercress for garnish

Combine all ingredients; chill. Serve in bowl surrounded by favorite crackers. Wonderful!
Makes about 3 cups.

Frances C. Wilkins, San Antonio, Texas

TEXAS PLACE:
The City of McAllen, nestled in the Rio Grande Valley, is known as the "City of Palms" due to the many palm trees that dot the landscape due to the subtropical climate of the area which produces blue skies and sunny days all year long! This climate attracts tremendous numbers of "Winter Texans" who live the rest of the year in the northern parts of the United States and Canada!

COWBOY TOSTADO DIP

2 lbs. lean ground chuck
1 large onion, chopped
2 (15 oz.) cans tomato sauce
  with tomato bits
1 (12 oz.) jar mild picante
  sauce

1 (6 oz.) jar hot taco sauce
1 (4 oz.) can chopped green
  chilies in juice
2 tsps. *or* to taste chili powder
1 cup sharp Cheddar
  cheese, grated

1 (4 oz.) can chopped black
  olives
Tostados

In large pan, brown meat and onions; stir to crumble; drain. Mix in next 5 ingredients; cover; reduce heat, and simmer an hour; stir occasionally. Transfer to serving dish, top with cheese and olives. Serve with tostados.

Makes 6 Texas Hearty cups!!   Gerry Ebner, Wichita Falls, Texas

TEXAS CAVIAR

2 (15 oz.) cans black-eyed
  peas, drained
1/2 cup green pepper, chopped
1/4 cup vegetable oil

1/4 cup red wine vinegar
1/2 cup purple onion, chopped
1/4 cup sugar
1 clove garlic, finely chopped

1/2 tsp. salt
Pepper to taste
Pita chips (page 10)

In large bowl, combine first 9 ingredients; stir to mix. Cover; refrigerate for 8-12 hours before serving. Drain. Serve with Pita Chips, and enjoy. In Texas, having black-eyed peas on New Year's Day ensures happiness all year long!

Makes 5-6 cups.   Jackie Spears, Dallas, Texas

DEVILICIOUS CHEESE BALL

2 (4 1/4 oz.) cans deviled ham
  spread
1 (4 oz.) pkg. dry ranch style
  dressing mix

1 (8 oz.) pkg. cream cheese
1/2 cup tomatoes, diced
1/2 cup green peppers, diced
2 cups Cheddar cheese, grated

1/2 cup pecans, chopped
Favorite crackers

In bowl, combine first 6 ingredients; refrigerate. Before serving, form into a ball, and roll in pecans. Surround with crackers.

Dee Danaher, GREAT FLAVORS OF TEXAS

TEXAS FACT:
The gemstone of the State of Texas is the beautiful Topaz!

SOMBRERO DIP

2 (8 oz.) pkgs. cream cheese,
  softened
1 cup picante sauce (page 99)
4 green onions, finely chopped

1 (2½ oz.) jar dried beef,
  finely chopped
1 tsp. cumin
½ tsp. oregano

Tortilla & Spicy Pita Chips
(below)

Blend all ingredients together; refrigerate. Serve with chips. Texas Spicy!!
Yields 3-4 cups.

Deanna Brown, Dallas, Texas

SPICY PITA CHIPS

2 (1 lb.) pkgs. pita bread
2 sticks unsalted butter,
  melted
2 Tbsps. garlic, minced

¼ tsp. ground cumin
½ tsp. fresh oregano, chopped
  (¼ tsp. dried)
¼ tsp. paprika

¼ tsp. red chili pepper
⅛ tsp. cayenne pepper
Dash of salt
Dash of white pepper

Cut each bread slice like pie into quarters to make 4 triangular shapes. Carefully pull each triangle apart at the fold to make 8 single chips. Mix butter with remaining ingredients. Place triangles in large bowl; add butter mixture; gently toss to coat triangles. Spread pitas in single layer on baking sheet; bake at 300° for 30 minutes or until crisp like croutons. Cool completely. Chips may be stored in airtight container for up to a week. Super with spreads and dips!
Yields about 148 chips.

Chef Nancy Beckham, BRAZOS CAFE, Dallas, Texas

Nancy owns the BRAZOS CAFE, which is well known in Dallas for its exceptional Southwestern Cuisine!

TEXAS BIG:
Dallas is home to four different churches that are each the largest church in its individual denomination in the world. They are the First Baptist Church, East Dallas Christian Church, Highland Park Methodist Church, and Highland Park Presbyterian Church.

BEST BAKED BASIL TOMATO SPREAD

16 small Roma tomatoes, cut lengthwise & stemmed
2/3 cup fresh basil

8 cloves garlic, minced
1/3 cup olive oil
Salt to taste

Loaf French bread, thinly sliced

Place tomatoes, cut sides up, in shallow baking pan. Sprinkle with basil and garlic; drizzle oil over all. Bake at 200° for 2-2½ hours; check occasionally; when done tomatoes will be shriveled, still moist, and not brown. Cool to room temperature; refrigerate. To serve, add salt; serve at room temperature with bread. Marvelous!

Serves 8. (Easily doubled)

"The tomatoes are also great as pasta or pizza toppings, with grilled cheese sandwiches, or in tossed green salads!"

Nancy Lemmon, Dallas, Texas

SHERRY CHEESE SPREAD

2 (3 oz.) pkgs. cream cheese, softened
1 cup sharp Cheddar cheese, shredded

4 tsps. sherry
1 tsp. curry powder
1/4 tsp. salt
8 ozs. chutney, chopped

4 green onion tops, sliced
Favorite crackers

Beat together cheeses and sherry; blend in curry and salt. On serving platter, spread mixture to ¼-inch thickness. Spread chutney on top; sprinkle with onion tops. Good!!

Yields about 3 cups.

Betsy Smith, Tyler, Texas

TEXAS FESTIVALS:
Tyler has a number of marvelous annual festivals! One is the East Texas Fair, an outstanding livestock event, which is held in late September and draws over 100,000 visitors! The Tyler Rose Festival is held every October. Another treat is the Azalea and Spring Flower Show held in late March and early April!

TEXAS BIG:
Tyler is the Rose Capitol of the World. The Tyler Municipal Rose Garden is the largest rose garden in the United States!

SOUTH TEXAS CHEESE ROLL

8 ozs. Velveeta
4 ozs. cream cheese, softened
Garlic salt to taste
1 bunch green onions & tops, chopped
1 medium jalapeno, chopped
1 Tbsp. picante sauce
Seasoned salt to taste
Seasoned pepper to taste
Fresh parsley for garnish, optional
Favorite crackers
Wax paper

Between 2 pieces of wax paper, roll Velveeta into thin rectangle; remove top layer of wax paper. Spread cream cheese evenly over Velveeta; sprinkle with garlic salt. Top with onions and jalapeno. Roll cheese from wide side to make log; remove wax paper. Top with picante sauce and seasonings. *Serves 8.*

Linda Sue Barnes, George West, Texas

WONDERFUL CHEESY HOT POT

1 round, firm, & unsliced loaf bread
2 cups Cheddar cheese, shredded
1 cup Monterey Jack cheese with jalapenos, shredded
2 (3 oz.) pkgs. cream cheese
1½ cups sour cream
1 cup ham or Italian sausage, cooked & diced
1 (4 oz.) cup green chilies, chopped & drained
1 (4.2 oz.) can black olives, chopped & drained
1 (2 oz.) jar diced pimentos, drained
1 tsp. Worcestershire sauce
Raw vegetables, bread sticks, & crackers for dipping

Slice off bread's top; reserve. Hollow out loaf's inside, leaving ½-inch thick shell; save interior bread. In bowl, combine cheeses and sour cream; add next 5 ingredients; mix well. Spoon cheese mixture into bread shell. Cover with reserved top. Tightly wrap loaf with 4 layers of aluminum foil; place on cookie sheet. Bake at 350° for an hour or until cheese has melted and heated throughout. Before serving, cube leftover bread for dipping. To serve, remove foil; transfer "hot pot" to platter; stir; surround with vegetables, etc., for dipping.
Makes approximately 8 super cups!

Marti Turner, Houston, Texas

TEXAS PLACE:
The Houston Underground is a four mile system of underground pedestrian tunnels that includes a marvelous variety of shops and restaurants!

WONDERFUL SAUSAGE CHEESE MOLD

2 lbs. hot bulk sausage, cooked & drained
1 lb. Velveeta
1 lb. Cheddar cheese, grated
1 lb. extra sharp Cheddar cheese, grated
6 jalapeno peppers, seeded & chopped <u>or</u> 1 (4 oz.) can chopped green chilies
Jalapeno jelly (below)
Favorite crackers

In large skillet, combine sausage and cheeses; cook over low heat until cheeses melt. Stir in peppers; pour into greased 10-cup mold; refrigerate. To remove from mold, place mold in hot water for 1-2 minutes. Turn onto plate. Spread jelly over mold. Enjoy!
Yields 10 cups.

Mary Martha Henderson, Lufkin, Texas

MRS. DEWOODY'S JALAPENO PEPPER JELLY

1/4 cup jalapeno peppers, <u>very</u> finely chopped
3/4 cup green bell peppers, <u>very</u> finely chopped
1 1/2 cups apple cider vinegar
6 1/2 cups sugar
1 (6 oz.) bottle liquid pectin
Green food coloring, optional

In saucepan, combine first 4 ingredients; bring to boil. Boil 5 minutes; remove from heat. Add liquid pectin and a little food coloring. Pour into sterilized jars; seal. Great served over cream cheese with melba rounds! For festive color change, use red bell peppers and food coloring.
Yields about 3 pints.

Jeanne Verlenden, GREAT FLAVORS OF TEXAS

TEXAS FACT:
Lufkin, located in the heart of East Texas' Piney Woods region, is home to many of Texas' vast lumber and wood products industries and to the Texas Forestry Association and Forestry Museum.

TEXAS FESTIVAL:
The Hush Puppy Olympics, featuring the Hush Puppy Cook-off, are held annually in Lufkin in May.

SUPER SHRIMP SPREAD

1 tsp. Worcestershire sauce	1 tsp. onion salt	1 cup celery, diced
1 tsp. horseradish	½ cup mayonnaise	1 lb. shrimp, cooked, peeled,
1 tsp. seasoned salt	½ cup Miracle Whip	& chopped
1 tsp. garlic powder	12 ozs. cream cheese	Triscuits & crackers

Combine first 8 ingredients; beat until smooth. Add celery and shrimp; stir. Chill 4-6 hours. Too Good!

Yields 5 cups.

Lela Windham, Houston, Texas

SHRIMP MONACO

18 jumbo shrimp, cleaned & peeled	3 garlic cloves, crushed	½ - ¾ cup Italian bread crumbs
¼ cup butter, melted	½ cup sherry	Sherry to taste
	½ - ¾ cup Parmesan cheese	

Saute shrimp in next 3 ingredients until shrimp are pink. Coat shrimp with ½ cup cheese and crumbs; put in baking dish; keep warm. To serve, sprinkle with more sherry, rest of cheese and bread crumbs; reheat to hot. Serve hot with party toothpicks.

Serves 6-8.

Jerry Earl, Austin, Texas

TEXAS BIG:
The majestic Texas State Capitol, located in Austin, is the largest state capitol building in the United States. Completed in 1888, the Capitol has 400 rooms and 18 acres of floor space!! The Texas Legislature financed its construction by trading 3 million acres of land in the Panhandle to the contractor with the best bid!

TEXAS NOTABLE:
Lady Bird Johnson, former First Lady and wife of President Lyndon Johnson, is well known in Texas for her philanthropy. Her National Wildflower Research Center is located in Austin. Its twofold purpose is to study and identify the thousands of wildflower species found in the United States and to act as a national information center for those Americans interested in the study of wildflowers indigenous to the United States.

FRESH BASIL CHEESE PUFFS

1 cup milk	1 cup flour	1½ cups Parmesan cheese,
1 stick butter	5 eggs	grated
1 tsp. salt	½ cup fresh basil, chopped	

In saucepan, over medium heat, bring milk, butter, and salt to boil; add flour; stir to mix. Turn heat to very low; cook 5 minutes, stirring. Pour into bowl; let heated mixture stand 5 minutes. Add eggs, one at a time, stirring until well blended; add basil and cheese. Place by tablespoons on greased baking sheet; bake at 375° until golden brown. Serve hot.

Serves 20.

Chef Randy Barnett, DARYL'S BY DESIGN, Dallas, Texas

TEAROOM CHEESE WAFERS

1 stick butter, softened	Pinch of paprika	Non-stick vegetable oil
1 cup flour	Pinch of cayenne pepper	
Pinch of salt	½ lb. Cheddar cheese, grated	

In bowl, mix together first 5 ingredients; add cheese; mix well. Spray baking pan with oil. Roll dough into 48 balls; press down lightly to form disks. Bake at 350° until brown on edges, about 10 minutes.

Makes 4 dozen.

"These are wonderful as appetizers, served with salads, and, of course, at tea time!"

**Chef David Wallace, MY PERSONAL CHEF, and
TYLER SQUARE ANTIQUE MALL TEAROOM, Tyler, Texas**

TEXAS FACT:
Texas, with more than 5,175 miles of lakes and streams, ranks second in the United States in the volume of inland waterways! Of these, Tyler and Tyler East Lakes are two that cover 4,800 acres and offer extensive recreational opportunities!

TORTILLA FINGERS

2 (8 oz.) pkgs. cream cheese, softened
1 bunch green onions & tops, thinly sliced
1 (4 oz.) can green chilies, chopped
1 (4.2 oz.) can black olives, chopped
1 (2½ oz.) jar pimento, chopped
18 flour tortillas (page 78)
Picante sauce (page 99) & Salsa (page 101) for dipping

Combine first 5 ingredients. Layer as follows: Spread cheese over 2 tortillas. Stack 1 cheese layered tortilla over the other, cheese side up. Top with another tortilla. Repeat process until have 6 separate stacks of 3 cheese filled tortillas. Cover each with plastic wrap; chill until firm. Cut tortillas into 2-inch long strips that are <u>no more</u> than ¾-inch wide or into small wedges (like a pie); chill. Serve same day made with sauces.
Yields 5-6 dozen.

Erlann Clark, Dallas, Texas

TEXAS BEST CHEESE PUFFS

2 (5 oz.) jars Old English Cheese Spread
2 sticks butter, softened
½ tsp. Tabasco
½ tsp. onion powder
½ tsp. Worcestershire sauce
1½ tsps. dill weed
1 tsp. beau monde seasoning, optional
1 loaf very thinly sliced white bread, crust removed

Blend well cheese and butter; add next 5 ingredients; mix well. Spread 3 slices of bread with cheese mixture; stack; cut stack into 12 small squares. Coat well sides of mini-squares with cheese mixture. Repeat process until cheese mixture is gone. Bake at 350° for 6-8 minutes or until lightly browned. These wonderful goodies freeze well; just bake frozen puffs at 350° for 10-12 minutes.
Yields 8-10 dozen.

Ann Knoebel, San Antonio, Texas

TEXAS BIG:
San Antonians love fiestas, and San Antonio has an annual festival schedule that is second to none! These popular events include the Great River Country Festival in January, San Antonio Festival in June, Texas Folklife Festival in August, and the Holiday River Festival in December. The pinnacle festival is Fiesta San Antonio which spans ten days during the last two weeks in April. Fiesta San Antonio features Pilgrimage to the Alamo, the Coronation of King Antonio, Fiesta Night Parade, balls, street dancing, and the marvelous series of "Nights in Old San Antonio!"

FATHER'S FRIED 'N STUFFED JALAPENOS

1 gal. can large, whole pickled jalapenos (1 jalapeno = 1 serving)	1/4 cup green pepper, diced	Salt & pepper to taste
	1/4 cup onion, diced	Beer
	3 eggs	Flour
1/2 stick butter, melted	1 cup bread, cubed	Hot oil, 4-6 inches deep
1/4 cup celery, diced	1 lb. crab meat	

Leaving stems attached, slice jalapenos down 1 side creating a zipper for each. Under running water, scoop out and discard insides of jalapenos. Turn peppers zipper side down on paper towels to dry. In skillet with butter, saute next 3 ingredients; add eggs and bread; gently mix in crab meat and seasonings; cook until mixture has consistency of soft scrambled eggs. Remove; cool. Stuff peppers until each is full and firm. To make batter, mix beer and flour in equal parts until thick. Holding jalapenos by stems, run them through batter; immediately, drop in oil. When peppers brown, remove; drain on paper towels. Serve immediately. Well Worth The Effort!

Serves 10-12. (Easily doubled)

"My father and I worked on this recipe for months in the mid 1970's. We came up with the beer batter before it became popular! Our recipe placed third in the SAN ANTONIO EXPRESS-NEWS COOKING CONTEST in 1979. I love this recipe because my father and I spent many lovely hours together working to get it exactly right!"

Jan Bennett Steger, GREAT FLAVORS OF TEXAS

TEXAS TREASURE:
Rich in south-of-the-border flavor, Laredo, Texas, is the major international crossing along the United States' border with Mexico. Since 1898, Laredo, uniquely, has honored George Washington with the Washington Birthday Celebration. This four day fiesta honors Washington as the first Western Hemisphere leader to free a New World country from the domination of European rule! This fiesta is celebrated on both sides of the border and includes parades, fireworks, dances, and an impressive coronation ceremony!

WONDERFUL ARTICHOKES

3 artichokes, stems
    & all points trimmed
1 cup red wine
2 cups chicken stock from cubes
2 small ripe tomatoes,
    coarsely chopped

1 tsp. dried basil
1/2 tsp. dried thyme
1/4 tsp. dried rosemary
1 jalapeno, halved
2 large garlic cloves, minced
2 medium shallots, chopped

1 tsp. lemon juice
1 Tbsp. soy sauce
1/4 tsp. sesame oil
1 Tbsp. olive oil
1/4 tsp. pepper

Place artichokes, bottom side down, in burner proof 1½-quart casserole. In bowl, mix together remaining ingredients; add to casserole; bring to boil on top of stove. Cover tightly; cook in 350° oven for 1¼-1½ hours depending on size of artichokes. Cool in liquid. For first course, serve cold in halves; as appetizer, serve quartered. Delightful!

Renie Steves, CUISINE CONCEPTS, Fort Worth, Texas

ZUCCHINI DELIGHTS

4-5 zucchini, thinly sliced
1 cup biscuit baking mix
1/2 cup onion, chopped
3/4 cup Parmesan cheese,
    grated

2 Tbsps. parsley flakes
1/2 tsp. salt
1/2 tsp. seasoned salt
1/2 tsp. dried oregano leaves
Dash of pepper

1/2 tsp. garlic powder
1/2 cup vegetable oil
4 eggs, beaten

In large bowl, mix well all ingredients. Spread in greased 9x13-inch pan; bake at 350° for 25 minutes or until golden brown. Cool slightly; cut into squares; serve warm.
Makes 4 dozen. (Freezes well)

RARE COLLECTION COOKBOOK, Junior League of Galveston County, Texas

TEXAS TREASURES:
Galveston's nostalgic trolley cars connect the beach at the sea wall to the historic Strand Bay area. The replica "1900 vintage" cars glide for 4½ miles along tracks much like those of Galveston's early days.

TEXAS TRASH

1 (18 oz.) box Alphabets	2 lbs. pecan halves	2 tsps. Tabasco
1 (18 oz.) box Cheerios	1 (10 oz.) bottle	4 Tbsps. garlic powder
1 (18 oz.) box Wheat, Rice,	Worcestershire sauce	1 lb. margarine
or Corn Chex	4 Tbsps. savory salt	2 cups bacon fat
1 (18 oz.) box Captain Crunch	4 Tbsps. celery salt	2 Tbsps. liquid smoke
2 (7 oz.) bags stick pretzels	4 Tbsps. chili powder	

Mix first 6 ingredients in large roasting pan. In saucepan, combine remaining ingredients; bring to boil. Pour over dry mixture, spreading evenly; mix well. Put in preheated 200° oven; stir every 20 minutes for 1½ hours. Then, test to see if dried mixture has absorbed liquid or is almost dry. Let cool well; store in 4 two pound coffee cans. Keeps indefinitely.

SOUTH PADRE ISLAND CEVICHE

1½-2 lbs. or more fresh firm	2 onions, chopped	Dash of vinegar
fish such as red fish, red	3 firm tomatoes, chopped	Fresh garlic to taste,
snapper, piggy perch,	1 jalapeno, chopped	chopped, optional
chopped	2 Tbsps. cooking oil,	Fresh cilantro to taste,
Juice of 12 limes	more if desired	optional

Marinate fish in lime juice, covered, in refrigerator for 3 days. In colander, thoroughly rinse juice off fish. Separately, combine remaining ingredients; taste; adjust seasonings; add fish. Good! *Serves 8-10.*

Zetta Fair, South Padre Island, Texas

Zetta owns PADRE STYLES, a lovely clothing store, located on South Padre Island!

TEXAS TREASURE:
110-mile-long Padre Island offers one of the last natural seashores in the United States! Each end of this narrow sand island is developing with parks and resorts. But in between, the National Seashore preserves an unblemished 80 mile stretch of the island's middle. Beachcombers may leisurely collect seashells, driftwood, and every now and then, prized glass floats washed in by the tides from distant lands such as the Orient or Portugal!

19

TEXAS COAST CRAB CAKES

1 lb. fresh crab meat, rinsed & cartilage removed or 1 lb. frozen crab meat, thawed
1 cup onion, finely chopped

1 tsp. dry mustard
1/4 tsp. cayenne pepper
1/4 cup mayonnaise
1 egg, beaten
1/4 cup dry bread crumbs

Vegetable oil for frying
1 cup dried bread crumbs
Parsley for garnish

In bowl, combine first 7 ingredients; shape into 8 cakes. Over medium heat in skillet, heat 1-inch deep oil. Coat each cake with dried crumbs; fry in hot oil until golden brown; drain on paper towels. Keep warm in 250° oven. Garnish and serve with Best Remoulade Sauce. *Yields 8 delicious crab cakes!*

BEST REMOULADE SAUCE

1 cup mayonnaise
2/3 cup creole style mustard or coarse grain mustard

1/3 cup vegetable oil
3 Tbsps. onion, finely chopped
3 Tbsps. celery, finely chopped

1 Tbsp. parsley, finely chopped
1/4 tsp. paprika

In blender, mix first 2 ingredients. With motor running, slowly pour in oil in steady stream. Blend in rest of ingredients; refrigerate. Good with crab and shrimp!
Makes 2 cups.

John C. Crank, Dallas, Texas

TEXAS BIG:
Fort Worth, affectionately called Cowtown by its residents, is home to BILLY BOB'S TEXAS, the largest "honky tonk" in the world! BILLY BOB'S TEXAS has 100,000 square feet and features concerts in the Showroom every Friday and Saturday nights and a sawdust covered dance floor that has 10,000 square feet where you can dance the two-step to live country western music!!

TEXAS FACT:
The Port of Houston is one of the top three seaports in the United States in total tonnage shipped! Houston is connected to the Gulf of Mexico by a 50 mile long shipping channel.

J & J CAMP CEVICHE

1 lb. white fish (trout, red snapper, flounder), skinned, veined, boned, & finely chopped
Juice of 8-10 fresh limes
2 cloves garlic, crushed

Salt & pepper to taste
2 cups sweet onion, finely chopped
1 cup ripe tomatoes, chopped & seeded

4-6 serrano or jalapeno peppers, seeded & finely chopped
1 cup fresh cilantro leaves, if available
Saltine crackers

Place fish in flat glass dish. Completely cover fish with lime juice. Add garlic; sprinkle with seasonings. Tightly cover; refrigerate 12 hours or more, stirring several times. Before serving, drain fish; return to dish. Add onions, tomatoes, and peppers; mix well. Refrigerate another 1-2 hours. To serve, add cilantro, adjust seasonings, arrange in chilled glass bowl surrounded by crackers. Super served in cocktail glasses, garnished with lettuce, cilantro sprigs, and lime wedges!
Serves 6-8. (Easily doubled)

"This is the perfect ceviche recipe developed through many 'trial and error' attempts at the J&J Camp at Pt. Mansfield, Texas, our favorite fishing village!"

Jim Bennett, Houston, Texas

TEXAS NOTABLE:
Sam Houston came to Texas in 1832 to fight for Texas' independence from Mexico. Houston became Commander-in-Chief of the Texan Army and successfully commanded Texans at the Battle of San Jacinto. In 1836, he became President of the Republic of Texas. After Texas became a part of the United States, he served both as a United States Senator and Governor of Texas. Houston's last battle was in opposition to Texas' secession from the Union at the start of the Civil War. He is one of Texas' great heroes, and his statue on the grounds of the State Capitol Building depicts Houston sitting proudly astride his horse.

HEARTY HILL COUNTRY PARTY MEATBALLS

1½ lbs. ground round
1 cup prepared bread crumbs
1 cup sweet pickle relish
2 eggs
2 tsps. onion, grated
1 tsp. cinnamon

2 Tbsps. brown sugar
½ cup milk
1 tsp. salt
1-2 Tbsps. cooking oil
2 cups catsup
½ cup brown sugar

1½ cups water
2 tsps. A-1 Steak Sauce
2 tsps. Worcestershire sauce
1 tsp. garlic powder

With electric mixer, blend well first 9 ingredients. Shape meat mixture into walnut-sized balls; brown in hot oil; set aside. To make sauce, in bowl, combine remaining ingredients. In skillet, combine meatballs and sauce; cook over low heat for 10-20 minutes. Serve hot with cocktail picks. Delicious Cold Weather Appetizer!
Serves 9-12.

Jean Williams, Wimberley, Texas

SPICY PECANS

3 Tbsps. butter
1½ tsps. salt

3 Tbsps. Worcestershire sauce
¼ tsp. cayenne pepper

3-4 dashes Tabasco
1 lb. pecan halves

In skillet, combine first 5 ingredients; cook over medium heat until melted. Stir in pecans; coat all well. Spread in single layer on baking pan with sides; bake at 300° for 20-25 minutes, turning every 5 minutes. Pecans are done when golden brown. Store in airtight container. Pecans freeze well. Wonderful!!

Anne Williams, Dallas, Texas

TEXAS PLACE:
Wimberley, a popular summer resort, is situated very picturesquely, in Texas' beautiful Hill Country. During the months between May and October, the first Saturday of each month is Market Day in Wimberley. Work produced by local artists is offered for sale along with antiques. Located just outside Wimberley is Pioneer Town, which has a collection of old buildings which replicate a nineteenth century western village.

SOUTH OF THE BORDER MARGARITAS

1 (6 oz.) can frozen limeade	*Ice*	*Lime wedges*
9 ozs. tequila	*⅛ lime, diced*	
2 ozs. triple sec	*Coarse salt*	

In blender, put first 3 ingredients; fill with ice; blend until smooth. Rub edges of glasses with lime; dip in salt. Add blended mixture; garnish with lime wedges. Enjoy!
Yields 6-8 (5-ounce) servings.

LONGHORN SANGRIA

1 (1 pt. + 8.5 ozs.) bottle Burgundy	*1½ ozs. Cointreau*	*1 (8 oz.) bottle marashino cherries, drained*
1 (10 oz.) bottle club soda	*Juice of 2 oranges, 1 lemon & 1 lime*	*Lemon, orange, & lime slices*
½ cup brandy	*3 Tbsps. sugar*	

In large pitcher or bowl, mix first 6 ingredients; chill. Garnish with cherries and fruit slices. Serve in tall glasses over ice.
Yields about 2 delicious quarts!

NECESSITIES AND TEMPTATIONS COOKBOOK, Junior League of Austin, Texas

NECESSITIES AND TEMPTATIONS, recently featured in both REDBOOK and GOOD HOUSEKEEPING, is the cookbook choice for the busy woman of the 1990's for it offers not only recipes with the fabulous flavors of Texas but also, uniquely, a complete kitchen reference guide!!

TEXAS NOTABLE:
Stephen F. Austin, known as the Father of Texas, came to Texas in 1821 and established several colonial settlements that were later to become the heart of the Republic of Texas. For 15 years, Austin's vision and courage guided the development of Texas, then part of Mexico. The City of Austin is named in his honor.

RODEO PUNCH

Juice of 12 lemons
4 cups sugar
1 qt. soda water

6 cups brandy
1 pt. peach liqueur
1 pt. rum

Fruit slices for garnish,
  optional
Ice

In saucepan, heat juice; add sugar; stir to dissolve; cool. In punch bowl, combine "sugared" juice and next 4 ingredients. Top with fruit; serve over ice. Enjoy!
Yields 35 crowd pleasing servings.

Mary Minter, Abilene, Texas

CHRISTMAS EVE PEPPERMINT PUNCH

1 gal. peppermint ice cream
  in scoops
2 qts. eggnog

2 qts. ginger ale
2 cups heavy cream

1 - 1½ cups peppermint
  candy, crushed

Put first 3 ingredients in punch bowl. Top with cream, then candy, and serve.
Yields 2 gallons that children love!!

Barbara House, Abilene, Texas

COW PUNCH

3 ozs. bourbon
1 oz. brandy

3 Tbsps. sugar
1 tsp. vanilla

2 cups milk
6-8 ice cubes

In blender, combine all ingredients until frothy, and serve. Marvelous!
Yields 1 quart.

Judy Willingham, Abilene, Texas

REAL TEXAS FOLK'S FACT:
Real Texans know that if a man's from Texas he'll tell you, and if he's not, why embarrass him by asking!

PINA COLADAS

1 (14½ oz.) can sweetened cream of coconut	1½ (14½ oz.) cans light rum	½ banana, optional
2 (14½ oz.) cans pineapple juice	Ice	
	Slice of pineapple	

In blender, mix first 3 ingredients; refrigerate. When ready to serve, put ice in blender to ¾ full; add coconut mixture to ½ full. Add pineapple slice and banana; blend. Serve in champagne glasses. Enjoy!

Serves 16.

Pam Corcoran, McAllen, Texas

TEQUILA SLUSH

| 1 (6 oz.) can frozen lime juice or fresh lime juice | 1 (6 oz.) can frozen orange juice | 1 qt. bottle lemon-lime soda |
| 2 (6 oz.) cans frozen limeade | 6 (6 oz.) cans water | ⅓-½ qt. tequila |

Mix all ingredients together; freeze. Thirty minutes before serving, stir mixture until slushy. This keeps indefinitely and can be frozen again. Truly a South Texas Treat!!

Yields 10-12 servings.

Cissy Owens, McAllen, Texas

BORDER BUTTERMILK

| 1 (6 oz.) can frozen pink lemonade or limeade | 1 (6 oz.) can tequila | Ice |

In blender, combine first 2 ingredients; fill with ice. Blend until slushy; serve in stemmed glasses. Good!

Serves 6-8.

Martha DeCou and Betty Lowell, Corpus Christi, Texas
FIESTA COOKBOOK, Junior League Of Corpus Christi

TEXAS FESTIVAL:
Buccaneer Days, held every spring in Corpus Christi, is a celebration of the Landing of Alonza Alverez de Pineda, who discovered Corpus Christi Bay in 1519. Some of the fun includes pirates' capture of City Hall, parades, bay front fireworks, sailboat regatta, a carnival, and racing pigs!

TEXAS MILK PUNCH

| ½ gal. vanilla ice cream, softened | ½ gal. milk
2 cups bourbon | Nutmeg to taste |

In serving or punch bowl, spoon ice cream. Add milk and bourbon; stir. Sprinkle with nutmeg. **Exceptional!**

Serves 25. (Easily doubled or halved)   Camille Warmington, Houston, Texas

GREEN LIZARD

| 1 (6 oz.) can frozen limeade
1 (6 oz.) can vodka <u>or</u> to taste | 20-30 fresh mint leaves
Ice cubes | 4-6 lime slices for garnish
4-6 mint sprigs for garnish |

In blender, combine first 2 ingredients; add mint. Fill blender to top with ice cubes; blend until slushy. Garnish, and serve immediately. **Wonderful Summertime Drink!**

Serves 6. (Easily doubled)

Mary Denny, San Antonio, Texas

GRINGO THIRST QUENCHER

| 1 (6 oz.) can frozen orange juice
1 cup milk | 1 cup water
½ cup sugar
1 tsp. vanilla | 10 ice cubes
Orange slices, halved for garnish, optional |

In blender, mix all ingredients until cubes are crushed, and mixture is slushy. Garnish, and serve immediately. **Refreshing!**

Serves 6.   Jean Fullmer, San Antonio, Texas

TEXAS TREASURE:
The Alamo, an abandoned Spanish mission, built in 1755, became in 1836 the "Cradle of Texas Liberty." In thirteen days of seige (Feb. 23-Mar. 6), 187 Texas volunteers defied a Mexican army of thousands led by the dictator, Santa Anna. Although the Alamo defenders died to the last man, cost to the Mexican Army was high. The brave men of the Alamo and their sacrifice became the rallying point for a united Texas, whose army led by Sam Houston thoroughly routed the Mexican Army at San Jacinto. Today, the Alamo, Texas' most famous shrine, located in midtown San Antonio, is open to the public 7 days a week.

GAMMIE'S BANANA PUNCH

6 cups water	1 (6 oz.) can frozen lemonade	5 ripe bananas, peeled
4 cups sugar	2¼ cups water	& crushed
1 (12 oz.) can frozen orange juice	1 (48 oz.) can pineapple juice	1 (2 liter) bottle lemon-lime carbonated soft drink

In saucepan, over high heat, combine first 2 ingredients; bring to boil; cool. Add next 5 ingredients; stir. Freeze mixture. Before serving, allow mixture to thaw for 30 minutes to an hour; add lemon-lime drink. Preparation time for this punch is about 10 minutes. Elegant Drink Loved By All!

Serves 50.   Janie Means, Dallas, Texas

BRUCE'S FRESH FRUIT PUNCH

2 cups sugar	2 cups pineapple juice	1 cup fresh strawberries
1 cup hot tea	1 qt. ginger ale	& orange slices
1 cup fresh lemon juice	1 cup fresh pineapple, chopped	Fresh mint for garnish
1 qt. orange juice		

Dissolve sugar in tea; cool. Add next 4 ingredients. Freeze enough of mixture to make block of ice to fit punch or serving bowl. Chill remaining mixture. When ready to serve, pour punch over ice block, stir in fresh fruit, and garnish. Delightful!

Serves 20-25.   Carolyn Bruce Rose, Dallas, Texas

HOT SPICED CIDER

| 3 ozs. "red hots" | 1 small lemon, quartered | ½ gallon apple cider |

Place candy and lemon in basket of percolator or drip coffee maker. Pour cider into percolator or reservoir; perk as you would coffee. Serve hot. Easy Cold Weather Drink!

Makes 8 cups.

Julie Johnson, College Station, Texas

TEXAS FACT:
Texas A&M University, located at College Station, was the state's first public institution of higher learning. Texas A&M is famous for its military Cadet Corps and noted for outstanding research in agriculture, engineering, nuclear technology, and salt and freshwater fisheries!

TEXAS PUNCH

6 whole cloves
4 sticks cinnamon
1 qt. apple cider

1 cup lemon juice
1 cup pineapple juice
3 cups orange juice

1 qt. ginger ale
1 qt. white wine, optional

In saucepan, simmer first 3 ingredients for 15 minutes. Chill for 6 hours. Then, add the 3 juices. Just before serving, add ginger ale and wine. Delicious!
Makes 3½ quarts.

Amy Levine, Austin, Texas

MEXICAN PUNCH

2 cups pineapple juice
2 cups orange juice

1 cup lemon juice
4 Tbsps. instant tea

2½ qts. hot water
2 cups sugar

Combine all ingredients; serve over ice. As good as it is easy!!
Makes 1 gallon of refreshing punch!

Charlotte Weberman, Dallas, Texas

ICED COFFEE NOG

½ cup instant non-fat dry
    milk powder

2 cups milk
2½ Tbsps. sugar

1 Tbsp. instant coffee
½ tsp. vanilla

Beat first 4 ingredients until smooth. Add vanilla. Chill; serve over ice cubes. Marvelous Summer Coffee Drink!
Serves 2. (Easily doubled)

Linda Wingartern, Fort Worth, Texas

REAL TEXAS FOLK'S FACT:
Every Texan knows that Texas occupies all of the Continent of North America except the small area set aside for the United States, Canada, and Mexico!

SOUPS, SALADS, AND SANDWICHES

SUE SIM'S APPLE SOUP

2 Tbsps. butter, melted	2 cups apple juice	1 cup yogurt *or* sour cream
1 lb. MacIntosh apples peeled, cored, & sliced	2 Tbsps. Apple Jack brandy	1¾ cups milk
2 Tbsps. butter	½ tsp. fresh nutmeg, grated	⅓ cup sugar
2 Tbsps. flour	Pinch of salt	1-2 Tbsps. fresh lemon juice
	Pinch of cinnamon	Cinnamon sticks for garnish

In skillet with butter, saute apples until begin to soften, about 3 minutes. Add rest of butter; melt; stir in flour; cook over low heat; stir constantly for 2 minutes. Gradually, stir in juice; add next 4 ingredients; bring to boil. Reduce heat; simmer until slightly thickened, about 5 minutes; stir constantly. Remove from heat; stir in yogurt; place half mixture into blender; puree until smooth; pour into bowl. Repeat process. Stir in next 3 ingredients; cover; refrigerate. Serve, at room temperature, topped with a cinnamon stick. Deliciously different!

Sue Sims, San Angelo, Texas

CALICO COUNTY'S CHEESE AND BROCCOLI SOUP

1 stick butter, melted	½ cup flour	1 (10 oz.) pkg. chopped frozen broccoli, thawed & drained
1 Tbsp. onion, grated	2 cups chicken broth	
1 stalk celery, finely diced	2 cups milk	
1 carrot, grated	4 ozs. Velveeta	Salt & pepper to taste

In saucepan, saute in butter next 3 ingredients until limp, about 2 minutes. Add flour; cook for a minute or until mixture is thick. Add broth and milk; stir until smooth. DO NOT BOIL! Add cheese; stir until melted. Add broccoli and seasonings; stir until blended.
Serves 6.

CALICO COUNTY RESTAURANT, Amarillo, Texas

CALICO COUNTY RESTAURANT is a super place to enjoy Texas' best down home cooking!!

TEXAS FACT & TEXAS BIG:
The city of San Angelo grew around the frontier site of Fort Concho which was established in 1867. San Angelo is home to the largest primary wool market in the United States!

COWBOY PINTO BEAN SOUP

2 cups pinto beans, rinsed
2 qts. water
3 cloves garlic, each halved
1 Tbsp. chili powder
1 tsp. salt or to taste
1 tsp. cumin
½-1 tsp. ground black pepper
¼ cup white rice, cooked
1 (10 oz.) can Ro-tel tomatoes
2 cloves garlic, finely minced
3 medium onions, finely chopped
1 cup bacon, cooked, chopped, & juices reserved
1 cup water
1 tsp. paprika
1 cup water, if needed

Put beans and water in large pot; add next 5 ingredients. Bring to boil; cover; cook over low heat for 2½ hours or until beans are tender; add water, if needed. To beans, add rice and Ro-tel. In bacon juices, saute garlic and onions until tender; add sauteed mixture, bacon and cup water to beans. Cover, simmer for an hour; stirring occasionally. Add last cup water, if needed, for "soupy" consistency. Add paprika; cook 5 minutes more; cool. For smoother soup, mix in blender. Reheat to serve. Mighty good!

Serves 8-12.   Frances Gilmore, San Antonio, Texas

SOPA DE ARROZ CON GALLINA
(Rice Soup with Chicken)

2 cups chicken, cooked & cut into bite-sized pieces
1 (6 oz.) box wild rice, uncooked
1 (1 lb.) pkg. frozen mixed vegetables
¼ tsp. sage
1 tsp. black pepper
4 (10½ oz.) cans chicken broth
⅛ cup sherry
1 tsp. dried parsley

Put all ingredients in 3-quart pot; simmer 2-3 hours. If needed, add more broth. The wild rice gives soup a little different flavor! Good to have on hand on a "too busy to cook" day!

Makes 2½-3 quarts. (Freezes well)

Dottie Peek, Austin, Texas

TEXAS FACT:
On June 21, 1845, in Austin, the Texas Congress in Special Session approved annexation to the United States. The United States Congress approved annexation on December 29, 1845, making Texas the 28th State of the Union. The new State of Texas' cattle and ranching industries grew rapidly after unification. This led to the creation of the cowboy image, the Texas Longhorn legend, the rodeo, and other symbols of the Western frontier!

FRIEND'S FRENCH ONION SOUP

4 cups onions, thinly sliced
5 Tbsps. butter
6 beef bouillon cubes
6 cups water

2 tsps. salt _or_ to taste
½ tsp. pepper
½ cup cognac _or_ brandy,
    optional

2 slices bread, toasted &
    quartered
5 ozs. Mozzarella _or_ Swiss
    cheese, grated

Saute onions in butter until golden brown. In pot, bring bouillon and water to boil. Add onions and seasonings; cover; simmer 1 hour. Before serving, add brandy; pour into 4-6 oven-proofed bowls. Top each with 2 toast quarters; cover with cheese; boil until bubbly.
Yields 4-6 hearty servings!

Dixie Van Eynde, San Antonio, Texas

GALVESTON CREAMY GREEN BEAN SOUP

1 (10 oz.) pkg. frozen green
    beans, thawed or ½ lb.
    fresh green beans
3 cups chicken stock
½ onion, cut into quarters

1 medium potato, cut into pieces
2 cloves garlic, minced
2 Tbsps. fresh dill weed
    (2 tsps. dry)
½ tsp. garlic salt

¼ tsp. pepper
Salt to taste
3 Tbsps. sour cream
1 Tbsp. fresh lemon juice

In saucepan, combine first 9 ingredients. Bring to boil; reduce to simmer until vegetables are tender, about 30 minutes. Adjust seasonings to taste. Place in blender (several batches); puree until smooth. Return to saucepan; add sour cream and juice. Heat to hot; over low heat. **Wonderful and Unique Soup!**
Serves 2-4. (Easily doubled)

RARE COLLECTIONS COOKBOOK, Junior League of Galveston County, Texas

TEXAS TREASURE:
The ELISSA is a square-rigged sailing ship built in 1878 and lovingly restored by the citizens of Galveston. A project of the Galveston Historical Society, the ELISSA was chosen to be part of a permanent exhibit at the Galveston wharves. Today visitors tour the ELISSA and watch a film, describing the tall sailing vessel's dramatic adventures on the high seas!

GOOD 'N QUICK TORTILLA SOUP

1 (14½ oz.) can tomatoes with juice
1 medium onion, chopped
1 clove garlic, finely chopped
2 Tbsps. cilantro, chopped

Pinch of salt
4 cups chicken broth, hot
6 corn tortillas, cut into thin strips (page 78)
Corn oil

4 ozs. Monterey Jack cheese, grated
1 large avocado, diced

In blender, blend first 5 ingredients until smooth. Pour into saucepan, stir in broth; bring to boil. Cover; simmer 20 minutes. Meanwhile, in skillet with oil 2-3 inches deep, fry tortillas until crisp; drain. In soup bowls, place equal number of strips; cover with cheese; pour soup over all. Top with avocado. Serve at once. Marvelous and Easy!

Serves 4-5.   Mary Denny, San Antonio, Texas

GRANDMA'S VEGETABLE GUMBO

½ medium onion, chopped
1½ cups okra, sliced
3 Tbsps. bacon fat or cooking oil

1 head cabbage, shredded & covered with water
¼ cup water

Pinch of sugar
Salt & pepper to taste
2 tomatoes, peeled

Saute onion and okra in oil until soft, but not brown. Drain cabbage; then, add cabbage and ¼ cup water to sauteed mixture; cover; simmer until cabbage is soft. Add rest of ingredients; bring to boil; stir. Cook 1-2 minutes; if needed, add a little water. Gumbo will be thick. Serve with Cheese 'N Chilies Cornbread (page 76).

Serves 4. (Easily halved or doubled)

"This recipe is an heirloom which comes from my husband's grandmother's kitchen. It is wonderful served as a main course or side dish with grilled beef, pork, and chicken!"

Mary J. Harty, Lubbock, Texas

TEXAS PLACE:
The Walk of Fame, located in Lubbock, honors Lubbock and West Texas natives who have made major contributions in the Entertainment Industry. Some of the honored West Texans include Mac Davis, Waylon Jennings, and Jimmy Dean. The museum features a life sized bronze statue of Lubbock's favorite son, rock and roll legend, Buddy Holly.

CAPTAIN MAX LUTHER'S FISH CHOWDER

3-4 lbs. redfish or red
   snapper, boned & cut into
   pieces 3-inches square
2 large potatoes, thinly sliced
1 large onion, sliced

1 (16 oz.) can tomatoes
1-2 bay leaves, crumbled
1 clove garlic, minced
Minced parsley, optional
1-2 lemons, sliced

4 slices bacon, fried crisp
   & crumbled
Salt & pepper to taste
¾ cup Bordeaux wine

In large pot, put layer of potatoes, onion, and tomatoes; then, layer fish, all spices, lemon and bacon; season. Add enough water to just cover ingredients. Cover; simmer until potatoes are tender. Before serving, add wine; simmer 1-2 minutes. An heirloom recipe, of which the original served over 200 people!

Makes about 4 quarts.

Mrs. Max J. Luther, III Corpus Christi, Texas
FIESTA COOKBOOK, The Junior League of Corpus Christi, Texas

GULF SHRIMP GUMBO

1½ cups celery, chopped
1 cup green onions & tops,
   chopped
¼ cup parsley, chopped
½ cup green bell pepper,
   chopped
1 cup okra, coarsely chopped

1 stick butter, melted
½ cup water
1 (20 oz.) can tomatoes,
   chopped
1 (8 oz.) can tomato juice
2 (10¾ oz.) cans cream of
   mushroom soup

4 ozs. mushrooms, sliced
1 cup cooked rice
1 cup shrimp, cooked & peeled
1 tsp. black pepper
¼ tsp. cayenne pepper
1 tsp. salt
1 tsp. gumbo file

In a pan, saute first 5 ingredients in butter and water until tender; add next 6 ingredients; stir. Simmer until blended. Add rest of ingredients; simmer for 15 minutes. Good served with crusty bread!

Serves 6.

Leslie Melson, Dallas, Texas

TEXAS FESTIVALS:
The Texas Jazz Festival, held in Corpus Christi in July, attracts famous musicians from all over the United States! The Bayfest Festival, in Corpus Christi in September, is a family festival on the bayfront and features a boat parade, sailboat regatta, windsurfing, and the "Anything-But-A-Boat-That-Will-Float" race!

PANHANDLE VEGETABLE BEEF 'N WINE SOUP

1 lb. beef, coarsely ground
3 onions, chopped
2 Tbsps. butter
3 cups beef broth
1 cup red wine

2 (1 lb.) cans tomatoes, chopped
1 cup potatoes, peeled & cubed
1 cup carrots, sliced
1 cup celery, sliced

1/4 tsp. thyme
1/2 tsp. basil
2 Tbsps. parsley, minced
Salt & pepper to taste

In saucepan, brown beef; drain. In skillet, saute onions in butter until soft; add onions and rest of ingredients to beef; bring to boil. Reduce heat; simmer for 1½ hours. Super Cold Weather Soup!
Serves 6-8.

Jo Randel, Panhandle, Texas

200 PLUS POTATO SOUP

6 large Irish potatoes, peeled & chopped
2 large yellow onions, chopped
Water

1/4 tsp. celery salt
White pepper & salt to taste
1 Tbsp. flour
1 Tbsp. butter

1 qt. milk
2 Tbsps. parsley for garnish, optional
Parmesan cheese for garnish

In large pot, cover potatoes and onions with water; bring to boil; cook, covered, until tender. Add next 2 ingredients. Mix flour with butter; add to potatoes a little at a time. Slowly add milk; stir constantly. Heat to hot. To serve, top with garnishes.
Serves 6.

"This recipe was given to me when I lived in France. It's so delicious and easy to make that I have prepared it over 200 times since moving back home!"

Frances Gilmore, San Antonio, Texas

TEXAS PLACE:
The Square House Museum, in Panhandle, is open to the public. Its purpose is to preserve West Texas' heritage.

RANCH COUNTRY CREAM OF ARTICHOKE SOUP

8 cups chicken broth	1/2 cup onion, finely chopped	1/4 tsp. thyme
1 bay leaf	1/2 cup celery, finely chopped	1 (14 oz.) can artichoke hearts
4-6 celery leaves	6 Tbsps. flour	2 egg yolks, beaten
Salt & pepper to taste	1/4 cup lemon juice	2 cups light cream
2 tsps. parsley flakes	1 bay leaf	Fresh parsley for garnish
1 onion, quartered	1 tsp. salt	Lemons, thinly sliced, for
6 Tbsps. butter, melted	1/4 tsp. pepper	garnish

In pot, simmer first 6 ingredients for an hour; set aside. In skillet with butter, saute onion and celery until soft; add flour; cook a minute; stir constantly. Add broth mixture and lemon juice; blend; add next 5 ingredients; cover; simmer for 20 minutes or slightly thickened. Remove bay leaf. To serve, heat to boil; remove from heat; blend in cream and egg yolks. For smoother consistency, puree in blender. Serve garnished, either hot or cold. A West Texas Treat!
Serves 8.

Kay Stewart, Ozona, Texas
DIAMONDS IN THE DESERT COOKBOOK, Ozona Woman's League

ROUND-UP STEAK SOUP

1 stick margarine, melted	1 1/2 cups carrots, sliced	1 (1 lb.) can tomatoes,
1 cup flour	1 1/2 cups celery, sliced	chopped with juice
2 qts. water	1 cup onion, chopped	4 Tbsps. instant beef bouillon
2 lbs. ground round	2 cups frozen mixed vegetables	1 tsp. black pepper

In large pot over medium heat, stir together margarine and flour to make smooth paste. Add water slowly; stir constantly. Separately, saute beef; drain; add to pot. Add rest of ingredients; bring to boil; lower heat. Simmer until vegetables are tender, about 2 hours.
Yields 4 quarts.

Dottie Peek, Austin, Texas

TEXAS PLACE:
Ozona, located in Southwest Texas, is known as "The Biggest Little Town in Texas" and is the largest unincorporated town in Texas. Ozona is in the heart of Texas' ranching country with sheep, goats, cattle, and horses being the prime agricultural products.

STRAWBERRY GAZPACHO

1 qt. ripe strawberries, stemmed & finely chopped
4 oranges, peeled, sectioned, & finely chopped
¼ cup celery, finely chopped
¼ tsp. fresh ginger, grated
¼ cup jicama (if available), finely chopped
1 Tbsp. fresh mint, grated
1-2 Tbsps. fresh onion, finely chopped
1 large red bell pepper, finely chopped
4 medium red tomatoes, peeled, seeded, & finely chopped
1 qt. orange juice
1-2 Tbsps. Balsamic vinegar
Fresh lime juice to taste
Sugar to taste
Mint leaves for garnish
Jalapenos, chopped for garnish

In large bowl, combine all ingredients; if needed, adjust to taste with lime juice and sugar; refrigerate. Serve cold, garnished. May make a day ahead. Super Brunch Dish!
Serves 10-12.   Sue Sims, San Angelo, Texas

WONDERFUL CREAMY MUSHROOM SOUP

1 cup onion, finely chopped
1 cup celery, finely chopped
4 Tbsps. butter, melted
1 lb. fresh mushrooms, rinsed & coarsely chopped
3 Tbsps. flour
4 cups beef bouillon
1½ cups heavy cream
White pepper to taste

In saucepan, saute onion and celery in butter until soft; add mushrooms; cook 3-4 minutes. Add flour; stir constantly; stir in bouillon; bring mixture to boil. Remove from heat; stir in cream and pepper. Enjoy!
Serves 6.   Helen Smith, Fort Worth, Texas

TEXAS BIG:
Texas sprawls over 267,000 square miles, which constitutes an area larger than most independent countries!

Texas has more than 250,000 miles of roads, streets, and highways, 624 miles of tidewater coastline, and 91 mountains that are at least 1 mile high!

VEGETABLE CHEESE SOUP OLE

4 cups water
1 cup onion, chopped
1 cup celery, chopped
1 cup carrots, sliced
4 medium potatoes, peeled & cubed
2 cups green cabbage, shredded
2 tsps. chicken bouillon granules
Black pepper to taste
1 (10¾ oz.) can cream of mushroom soup
1 (10¾ oz.) can cream of chicken soup
1 (1 lb.) pkg. Mild Velveeta Mexican cheese, cubed
½ cup half & half
Parsley for garnish

In large pot with water, cook next 5 ingredients until tender. Add next 4 ingredients, stirring constantly. Over low heat, add cheese a little at a time; stir until melted. Before serving, add half and half; garnish. For tangier soup, substitute Hot Velveeta Mexican cheese for mild.
Serves 6-8. (Easily doubled or halved)

"This is my own recipe, derived from combining various cheese soup recipes. It is our family's favorite!"

Carolann Gerescher, San Antonio, Texas

YELLOW PEPPER GAZPACHO

6 yellow bell peppers, seeded & finely chopped
2 cucumbers, peeled & finely chopped
1 garlic clove, minced
¾ purple onion, finely chopped
4 tomatoes, peeled & finely chopped
2 cups chicken bouillon
¼ cup white wine vinegar
2 Tbsps. capers, drained
Salt & pepper to taste

In bowl, combine first 5 ingredients. Add rest of ingredients; stir; season to taste. Cover; chill well before serving. Simple and Excellent!
Serves 6. (Easily doubled or halved)

"I sometimes serve this elegant soup in the yellow pepper shells. When doing this, I cut a little off the bottom of each pepper so that it will sit evenly on each plate."

Claudia Erdmann, Dallas, Texas

Claudia is a very popular caterer in Dallas!

ALWAYS REQUESTED CORNBREAD SALAD

1 9x13-inch pan cooked cornbread, crumbled
1½ cups mayonnaise
2 cups celery, sliced
1 green pepper, seeded & chopped
¾ cup green onions, chopped
1 (5 oz.) jar green olives & pimentos, drained, rinsed, & chopped
¾ cup pecans, toasted & chopped
2 large tomatoes, chopped
1 tsp. sage
Pepper to taste
10 slices bacon, fried crisp & crumbled
1 jalapeno pepper, seeded & chopped

In bowl, combine all ingredients. Refrigerate 3-4 hours before serving. Wonderful!
Serves 12.

"This salad was served at the LA FEMME DU MONDE ANNUAL SALE, and everyone requested the recipe!"

Sally Brice, Dallas, Texas

ANN'S FROZEN FRUIT SALAD

1 (10 oz.) pkg. frozen strawberries, drained & 2 Tbsps. juice reserved
1 (10 oz.) can crushed pineapple, drained
2 (3 oz.) pkgs. cream cheese, softened
1 cup mayonnaise
1 cup pecans, chopped
1½ cups miniature marshmallows
½ pt. whipping cream, whipped

Combine first 3 ingredients; add rest of ingredients; mix well. Spoon into individual salad molds; freeze. Serve on lettuce cup. Delicious and a pretty pale pink color!
Serves 12-16 (depending on individual mold size).

"These are great when serving a crowd! They freeze well and can be a last minute time saver!"

Helen Fairchild Clement, Native of Houston, Texas

TEXAS FACT:
Texas, Hawaii, and Vermont share the distinction of being the only states in the United States that were once independent republics! Since 1519, six different flags have flown over the land called Texas. They are the flags of Spain, France, Mexico, the Republic of Texas, Confederate States of America, and United States!

ARTICHOKE RICE SALAD

1 (10 oz.) pkg. chicken
  flavored rice & vermicelli
  mix; prepared per pkg.'s
  directions (omit butter),
  & cooled
1 (4 oz.) jar diced pimentos,
  drained

½ cup green pepper, chopped
2 green onions & tops,
  chopped
1 (6 oz.) jar marinated
  artichokes, drained, juice
  reserved & chopped

¾ cup slivered almonds,
  toasted
1 tsp. curry powder
⅓ cup mayonnaise
Reserved artichoke marinade

Combine rice with next 5 ingredients. Separately, mix rest of ingredients; stir into rice. Cover; refrigerate. Serve on lettuce cups. Divine!
Serves 6-8.

Jane Ferguson, Fort Worth, Texas

HELEN CORBITT'S ASPARAGUS AND AVOCADO SALAD

1 ripe avocado, peeled &
  thinly sliced lengthwise
Fresh lemon juice
1 head red lettuce, washed &
  crisped

8 spears fresh asparagus,
  cooked & chilled
4 slices bacon, cooked crisp,
  drained, & crumbled
1 Tbsp. capers

2 Tbsps. lemon juice
⅓ cup salad oil
Salt & cracked pepper
Slivered red bell pepper

Shower avocado slices with juice. Arrange slices on lettuce; cover with asparagus, bacon, and capers. Mix 2 tablespoons lemon juice with salad oil. Pour over all. Season to taste. Top with red pepper slivers for a festive, holiday look!
Serves 4.

Jim Augur, Dallas, Texas

TEXAS FACT:
Commercial vegetables are grown in over 200 counties in Texas. Hidalgo County, located in the lush Rio Grande Valley, leads all counties in Texas in the number of vegetables harvested!

BEST EVER CHICKEN AND WILD RICE SALAD

*⅔ cup uncooked wild rice,
   cooked per pkg.'s
   directions & cooled*
½ cup mayonnaise
3 Tbsps. milk
2 Tbsps. lemon juice

*3 cups chicken, cooked & cut
   into ½-inch pieces*
¼ cup onion, finely chopped
*1 (8 oz.) can water chestnuts,
   drained & sliced*

Salt & pepper to taste
2 cups seedless grapes, halved
1 cup cashew nuts
6 lettuce leaves, rinsed

In bowl, combine first 8 ingredients; cover; refrigerate. Chill well. Before serving, stir in grapes and nuts; serve on lettuce leaves. Excellent!

Serves 6. (Easily doubled)   Leigh Shamburger, Dallas, Texas

BEST PASTA SLAW

*6 ozs. curly macaroni, cooked
   in chicken broth & drained*
1 medium cabbage, shredded
*6 green onions & tops,
   chopped*

1 carrot, grated
Salt & pepper to taste
¼ cup apple cider vinegar
½ cup vegetable oil
2 tsps. sugar

½ tsp. Dijon mustard
*1 cup slivered almonds,
   toasted*
⅓ cup sesame seeds, toasted

In bowl, combine first 5 ingredients. Separately, combine vinegar with next 3 ingredients. Toss vinegar mixture with pasta; chill well. To serve, toss with almonds and sesame seeds. Great Pasta Dish!

Charlotte Brunette, Wichita Falls, Texas

TEXAS TREASURES:
The real cowboys of Texas still ride the fence line, "punch" cattle, and "break" wild horses. They work on Texas ranches such as Tongue River Ranch and U Lazy S Ranch. Ranches such as these conjure up images of endless pastures, thousands of heads of cattle, and cowhands drenched in sweat, dust, and the smell of rawhide! What do these cowboys do when they get a few days off in August? They flock to the annual Texas Ranch Roundup held in Wichita Falls. Here, these cowboys compete as teams representing their ranch, with the winning team and ranch owning the bragging rights to "The Best Ranch in Texas." That is a title that is dear to the heart of any working cowboy!

COBB SALAD

1 large head Romaine, rinsed & cut into bite-sized pieces
8 slices bacon, cooked & crumbled
1/4 lb. blue cheese, crumbled

3 tomatoes, peeled & cut in 1/2-inch pieces
2 avocados, peeled & cut in 1/2-inch pieces

2 eggs, hard-boiled & finely chopped
4 strips pimento
Cobb Salad Dressing

In serving bowl, put lettuce; arrange next 6 ingredients in "spoke wheel fashion" on top; cover; refrigerate. To serve, bring salad to table; toss with dressing.
Serves 6.

COBB SALAD DRESSING

1/2 cup salad oil
1/4 cup red wine vinegar
1/4 tsp. sugar

1 tsp. lemon juice
1 garlic clove, whole
1/4 tsp. salt

Fresh ground pepper to taste

In jar, combine all ingredients; shake well; refrigerate. To serve, remove garlic clove.

"This is my variation of a salad made famous by Helen Corbitt, the Texas cooking legend! It makes a beautiful presentation!"

Martha Len Nelson, Denton, Texas

CONSERVATION PISTACHIO SALAD

1 (3¾ oz.) box pistachio pudding mix
1 (5½ oz.) can crushed pineapple with juice

1 (8 oz.) container Cool Whip
1 (11 oz.) can mandarin oranges, drained
1/2 cup nuts, chopped

1-2 kiwi & 8-10 strawberries, sliced for garnish, optional

Combine well first 3 ingredients. Fold in oranges and nuts; chill until set. Serve in crystal bowl.
Serves 8-10. (Easily doubled)

"This recipe is in the SAN ANTONIO CONSERVATION SOCIETY'S COOKBOOK. It is fast and easy and can be a dessert too! The green color makes it a festive Christmas or St. Patrick's Day dish."

Lady Cleo Bischoff, San Antonio, Texas

CHUTNEY CHICKEN SALAD

1 cup mayonnaise
1/2 cup (or to taste) chutney
1 tsp. curry powder
2 tsps. lime peel, grated
1/4 cup lime juice
1/2 tsp. salt

4 cups (white meat) chicken, cooked
2 (12 oz.) cans pineapple chunks, drained
2 cups celery, diagonally sliced

1 cup green onions & tops, sliced
1/2 cup whole blanched almonds, toasted
Crisp lettuce

Combine well first 6 ingredients; add next four ingredients; chill. To serve, mix in almonds; arrange salad on a bed of lettuce. An Absolutely Fabulous Chicken Salad!
Serves 6-8.

Mary Denny, San Antonio, Texas

CHICKEN SALAD SUPREME

6 chicken breasts, skinned, boned, cooked, & cubed
2 eggs, hard-boiled & chopped
2 cups salad croutons (page 49)
1/3 cup onion, finely chopped

1 cup mayonnaise
2 Tbsps. mustard
1 tsp. celery seed
1 tsp. oregano
1 tsp. Tabasco
1/2 tsp. paprika

1/4 tsp. pepper
Dash of cayenne pepper
1/4 tsp. dill weed

In bowl, combine first 4 ingredients. In another bowl, combine remaining ingredients; stir well to blend; add to chicken mixture. Stir gently to combine. Chill well. Very Delicious!!
Serves 8.

Jan Michie, Argyle, Texas

TEXAS NOTABLE:
Gail Borden (1801-1874) was a Texas surveyor and patriot and the inventor of condensed milk. He obtained a patent in 1856 for his discovery that milk could be condensed by evaporation. He was the founder of Borden Milk Company and has the distinction of having a Texas county, Borden, named for him as well as the only town in the county which is named Gail!

43

ELOISE'S BEST BROCCOLI SALAD

4 cups raw broccoli florets, chopped
8 slices bacon, cooked & crumbled

1/4-1/2 cup raisins
1 cup mayonnaise
1/4 cup sugar
3 Tbsps. vinegar

1/2 cup purple onion, chopped
1/2-3/4 cup slivered almonds, optional

In bowl, mix well all ingredients. Toss; chill well; serve. Just that simple!
Serves 6-8.
Eloise Erwin, Austin, Texas

FAVORITE FRUIT SALAD

1 (15½ oz.) can pineapple chunks, drained
1 (11 oz.) can mandarin oranges, drained

4-5 bananas, sliced
3-4 apples, coarsely chopped
1/2-1 cup pecans, chopped

6-8 maraschino cherries, optional

In bowl, mix all ingredients; gently toss. To serve, pour dressing (below) over fruit; gently mix. Use cherries for livelier color.
Serves 4-5.

FAMILY'S FAVORITE DRESSING

1 egg, well beaten
2 Tbsps. vinegar

1/2 cup sugar
Pinch of salt

1/2 pt. whipping cream, whipped

In saucepan over medium heat, combine first 4 ingredients. Reduce heat to low; cook; stir constantly until mixture thickens; cool. Just before serving, fold in whipped cream.
Makes about 1½ cups.

"This dressing will enhance all kinds of fruit combinations! The recipe has been a favorite in our family since its invention over 100 years ago!!"

Sug Zowarka, San Antonio, Texas

REAL TEXAS FOLK'S FACT:
Real Texas Folk know that the United States without Texas would look like a Boston Terrier with only three legs!

FIESTA CORN SALAD

3 (10 oz.) pkgs. frozen corn,
   slightly cooked
4 medium tomatoes, diced
6 green onions, finely sliced
2 green peppers, seeded & diced

1 red pepper, seeded & diced
8 ozs. Monterey Jack cheese,
   diced
¼ cup olive oil
¼ cup red wine vinegar

1 Tbsp. chili powder
1 tsp. cumin
¼ cup cilantro, chopped

In bowl, combine all ingredients; let stand an hour. Best served at room temperature. If refrigerated, remove an hour before serving. Easy and Wonderful!

Serves 8-10.
                                                         Ginger Carlin, Dallas, Texas

FIESTA TOSSED SALAD

½ cup slivered almonds
3 Tbsps. sugar
½ head Iceberg lettuce,
   washed & torn

½ head Romaine lettuce,
   washed & torn
1 cup celery, chopped

2-4 green onions & tops,
   chopped
1 (11 oz.) can mandarin
   oranges, drained

In pan over medium heat, cook almonds and sugar; stir constantly until almonds are coated and sugar dissolved; cool. Store in airtight container. Mix next 4 ingredients; toss; chill. To serve, add oranges and almonds; toss. Add dressing (below); toss again.

Serves 4-6.

DAISY'S DRESSING

½ tsp. salt
Dash of pepper

¼ cup vegetable oil
2 Tbsps. sugar

2 Tbsps. vinegar
Dash of Tabasco

In jar, mix well all ingredients. Chill 2-3 hours before using. Good!

Makes about half a cup.

Daisy Brown, San Antonio, Texas

TEXAS FACTS:
The name Texas comes from tejas, the Indian word meaning friend. The motto of the State of Texas is Friendship.

45

GREAT FLAVORS' FRESH FRUIT SALAD

*1 small watermelon, seeded
& cut into bite-sized pieces*
*1 large cantaloupe, seeded &
cut into bite-sized pieces*
*1 pineapple, skinned, cored
& cut into bite-sized pieces*
1 cup tequila
½ cup orange juice
½ cup powdered sugar
¼ cup grenadine syrup
*1 pt. blueberries, rinsed &
drained*

Put first 3 fruits in large bowl. Separately, mix together next 4 ingredients; gently mix into fruit. Cover; refrigerate (up to 12 hours). To serve, drain fruit; fold in blueberries. A delicious, wonderful way to serve fruit that can be prepared ahead!
Serves 10-12.

Sherry Ferguson, GREAT FLAVORS OF TEXAS

GRILLED CHICKEN SALAD

½ cup vegetable oil
¼ cup lemon juice
1 Tbsp. paprika
2 Tbsps. Worcestershire sauce
2 Tbsps. vinegar
1 tsp. salt
2 tsps. sugar
2 tsps. garlic salt
*4 chicken breasts, skinned &
boned*
4 ears fresh corn
Olive oil
1 purple onion, diced
1 red bell pepper, diced
1 green bell pepper, diced
Dijon Vinaigrette, (below)

To make marinade, mix first 8 ingredients. Pour over chicken; refrigerate overnight. Drain chicken; grill over hot coals until done, about 5 minutes a side. Rub corn with olive oil; grill until done, about 10 minutes. Scrape corn off cob. Slice chicken into strips. In bowl, mix chicken, corn, and rest of ingredients with vinaigrette. Distinctly Texas Dish!
Serves 4.

DIJON VINAIGRETTE

*2 Tbsps. white wine
vinegar*
1 tsp. Dijon mustard
¼ tsp. ground cumin
¼ cup olive oil

In bowl, mix well all ingredients. Toss with chicken.

Ginger Carlin, Dallas, Texas

TEXAS PLACE:
The Dallas Theatre Center, in Dallas, is of great architectural note because it is the renowned American architect, Frank Lloyd Wright's, single direct contribution to the dramatic stage!

HOUSTON VEGETABLE SALAD SCRAMBLE

1 (16 oz.) can whole green beans
1 (8 oz.) can red kidney beans
1 (7 oz.) can pitted ripe olives
1 (6 oz.) can button mushrooms
1 (4 oz.) can pimentos
1 (15 oz.) can artichoke hearts
1 medium onion, thinly sliced & separated into rings
1½ cups celery, diagonally sliced
¼ cup parsley, chopped
2 Tbsps. capers, drained & rinsed

Drain, rinse, and dry first 6 ingredients. In bowl, mix well first 8 ingredients. Pour marinade (below) over all; mix. Marinate overnight; stir occasionally. To serve, top with parsley and capers. Enhances beef and pork dishes!
Serves 12.

MARY'S MARINADE

¼ cup tarragon vinegar
1 tsp. salt
1 tsp. ground pepper
1 tsp. sugar
¼ tsp. Tabasco
½ cup salad oil
1 Tbsp. Fines Herbes

In glass jar, shake vigorously first 5 ingredients. Add rest of ingredients; shake to blend.
Makes about 1 cup.

Mary Wilson, Houston, Texas

LONE STAR POTATO SALAD

8 potatoes, skinned, boiled, cooled & chopped
6 eggs, hard-boiled, cooled & chopped
4-6 stalks celery, chopped
¼ cup sweet pickle relish
2 Tbsps. Kraft Honey French Dressing
Lowery's Seasoned Salt & pepper to taste
1 cup mayonnaise or to taste

In bowl, combine potatoes and eggs. Add rest of ingredients in order listed; gently mix. That easy and good!
Serves 10-12.

Linda Smith, Austin, Texas

TEXAS FESTIVAL:
A major annual event is the Aqua Festival, which is held in Austin for ten days in August. The festival features parades, pageants, and water-related contests that are centered around Austin's Town Lake.

MARVELOUS PEPPERONI PASTA SALAD

1 lb. large pasta shells	1/4 cup red wine vinegar	1/4 cup Parmesan cheese,
6 ozs. pepperoni, cut into thin	1 tsp. Dijon mustard	grated
strips	1 garlic clove, minced	Juice of 1 lemon
1 red bell pepper, seeded &	1 tsp. anchovy paste,	1 cup olive oil
cut into thin strips	optional	Crisp lettuce

In saucepan, cook pasta in boiling water until tender; drain; rinse in cold water; drain again. Toss with next 2 ingredients; chill. In blender, mix wine vinegar and next 5 ingredients. With blender on, slowly add oil; blend until smooth. Pour over pasta mixture; toss until moistened; refrigerate. Serve over lettuce.
Serves 6.

Trina Ligon, Dallas, Texas

PRETTY BUTTERMILK SALAD

1 (15 1/4 oz.) can crushed	2 cups buttermilk	Cool Whip, lime & orange
pineapple with juice	1 (4 oz.) carton Cool Whip	slices for garnish
1 (6 oz.) pkg. jello, apricot		
or lemon-lime		

In saucepan, heat first 2 ingredients until jello dissolves; cool. Add buttermilk; mix well. Fold in Cool Whip. Put in glass bowl; chill until set. Serve garnished.
Serves 8 deliciously!

Genie Calgaard, San Antonio, Texas

TEXAS NOTABLE:
Author Katherine Anne Porter, born in the South Texas town of Indian Creek, won the Pulitzer Prize and National Book Award for THE COLLECTED STORIES OF KATHERINE ANNE PORTER. Her other works include SHIP OF FOOLS, FLOWERING JUDAS AND OTHER STORIES, NOON WINE, and PALE HORSE, PALE RIDER.

SOUTHWESTERN SHRIMP CAESAR

2-3 heads Romaine, washed
*   & torn into bite-sized pieces*
Caesar Salad Dressing
*   (below)*

1 cup fresh Parmesan cheese,
*   grated*
Spicy Croutons (below)

20 shrimp, cooked, peeled,
*   cleaned, & halved*
*   lengthwise*

Toss Romaine with dressing and ¼ cup cheese; divide into serving sizes; place on plates. Sprinkle rest of cheese on individual salads. Sprinkle croutons on top; garnish each with 4 shrimp halves. Grilled chicken may be substituted for shrimp. Excellent!
Serves 10.

CAESAR SALAD DRESSING

1 egg
1½ tsps. garlic powder
2 tsps. anchovy paste, optional
1½ tsps. cumin
½ cup fresh cilantro

½ tsp. seasoning salt
1 tsp. white pepper
½ tsp. chili powder
1½ tsps. Dijon mustard
Juice of 1 lemon

2 cups olive oil
½ cup Parmesan cheese,
*   grated*

In blender, mix first 10 ingredients. With blender on, add oil in a slow, thin stream. If desired, thin with a little water. Add cheese; blend for 15 seconds.
Makes 3 cups.

SPICY CROUTONS

2 sticks butter, melted
¼ tsp. cayenne pepper

1 Tbsp. garlic powder
1 Tbsp. parsley flakes

1 loaf bread, cubed

Mix well first 4 ingredients; toss with bread. Spread on baking sheet; bake at 375° until golden brown, about 15 minutes. Wonderful in other green salads too!
Yields 4-5 cups.

Randy Barnett, DARYL'S BY DESIGN, Dallas, Texas

SOUTHWEST SPINACH SALAD

1 (1 lb.) pkg. spinach, stemmed, washed, & torn

4-5 ozs. marinated, grilled chicken breast (page 46), sliced in strips

2 cups Cheddar cheese, grated

2 cups Mozzarella cheese, grated

Sliced mushrooms for garnish, optional

Bean sprouts for garnish, optional

Divide spinach into 4 equal parts; place on 4 plates. Layer with chicken, then cheeses. Top with mushrooms, sprouts, and a good vinaigrette (page 46).
Serves 4.

David Lewis, JOHN HENRY'S RESTAURANT, Wimberley, Texas

SUMMERTIME RICE SALAD

1 cup white rice, cooked per pkg.'s directions

1 (10 oz.) pkg. frozen peas, cooked per pkg.'s directions

4 Tbsps. onion, chopped

1/2 cup sliced mushrooms, drained

1/2 cup cucumber, chopped

1 cup Miracle Whip mixed with 1/2 cup Italian Dressing

Sliced cucumbers for garnish

To rice, add next 4 ingredients; toss with dressing mixture. Chill several hours for flavors to blend.
Serves 6-8.

"This salad makes a nice substitute for potato salad at picnics and summer suppers!"

Genie Calgaard, San Antonio, Texas

TEXAS PLACE:
Trinity University is an independent, nonsectarian, coeducational, and mainly liberal arts university located on a 113-acre skyline campus in San Antonio, the United State's ninth largest city. The enrollment is currently and will remain approximately 2,500 students.

TEXAS SHRIMP WITH THREE GRAIN SALAD

1/4 cup raisins
1/4 cup tea, warmed
2 qts. water
1/3 cup barley, uncooked
2 slices ginger, quarter-sized
1 tsp. orange peel, grated
1 tsp. salt

1/3 cup long grain rice, uncooked
1/3 cup kasha, if available, uncooked
8 scallions, chopped
1/2 cup broccoli flowerets, cooked & in tiny pieces
1 Tbsp. fresh mint, chopped

1 Tbsp. fresh cilantro, chopped
1 tsp. fresh ginger, finely minced
Savory Shrimp
Rio Grande Citrus Dressing
Orange & grapefruit sections or cilantro sprigs for garnish

Soak raisins in tea for 20 minutes; drain. In 3-quart pot, bring water to boil; add next 4 ingredients; gently boil 8 minutes. Add rice and kasha; boil 8 minutes. Remove from heat. Drain; fluff with a fork; cool; remove ginger. Separately, combine raisins, cooked grains, and next 5 ingredients. Cover, chill. Gently combine 1/2 cup dressing with grains. To serve, spoon tablespoon of dressing on plate; arrange shrimp on top; place salad on opposite side of plate; garnish.

SAVORY SHRIMP

3 Tbsps. shrimp seasoning   *1 1/2 lbs. large shrimp, uncooked*

In pot, bring 2-quarts water to boil. Add shrimp; remove from heat; let stand 5 minutes; drain. Peel and clean shrimp. Chill.

RIO GRANDE CITRUS DRESSING

8 Tbsps. brown sugar, packed
2 Tbsps. Dijon mustard
2 Tbsps. orange juice
1 1/2 Tbsps. grapefruit juice
1 1/2 tsps. white wine vinegar

1 Tbsp. concentrated orange juice
1/2 tsp. prepared horseradish
1/2 tsp. paprika
1/4 tsp. curry powder

1/4 tsp. salt
1/8 tsp. pepper
1/3 cup mayonnaise
2 Tbsps. corn oil

In pan over low heat, combine first 11 ingredients; stir; bring to boil. Remove from heat; cool 5 minutes. In blender, combine mixture and mayonnaise; slowly add oil.

Renie Steves, CUISINE CONCEPTS, Fort Worth, Texas

This wonderful recipe with a very definite flavor of Texas, won Second Place in Best Foods All American Salad Toss Up in 1990!

CORPUS CHRISTI CRAB BURGERS

1 cup crab meat	½ cup Cheddar cheese,	4 small hamburger buns, split
¼ cup celery, minced	shredded	& buttered
½ cup mayonnaise		

Combine first four ingredients; spread on buns; broil. That easy! Also a wonderful appetizer served with melba rounds!

Serves 4-6.

DAY BEFORE FOOTBALL FEED

3 lbs. chuck roast & 3 cups	2 Tbsps. vinegar	1 Tbsp. Worcestershire sauce
water	1 (14 oz.) bottle catsup	½ cup stock from cooked meat
1 onion, chopped	1 tsp. prepared mustard	Hot rolls or buns, heated
½ cup celery, chopped	4 tsps. lemon juice	
2 Tbsps. butter	2 Tbsps. brown sugar	

Stew chuck in water until meat falls apart, about 2½-3 hours; if needed, add more water. Shred cooked meat; remove gristle. To make sauce, saute onion and celery in butter; add next 6 ingredients; cook 10 minutes. Mix meat, stock, and sauce; refrigerate. Before serving, heat slowly; serve with rolls to make Sloppy Joe sandwiches. Serve with green salad (page 45) and a pot of beans (page 81). These make great fare after a Saturday of football watching! Make the day before to allow flavors to mingle!

Serves 8-10.

Marjorie Prichard and Frances Giddens
FIESTA COOKBOOK, The Junior League of Corpus Christi, Texas

FIESTA captures the hospitality, gaiety, gusto, and uniqueness of the South Texas area around Corpus Christi! The Junior League of Corpus Christi has sold over 520,000 of the cookbooks since first publishing FIESTA in 1973!!

CONFETTI SANDWICH

9 eggs, hard-boiled & chopped
1/4 cup sour cream
1/3 cup fresh spinach, chopped
1/2 cup carrots, shredded

1/2 cup stuffed olives, chopped
6 English muffins, split & toasted
Butter

1 cup Cheddar cheese, grated
8 slices bacon, fried crisp & crumbled

In bowl, combine first 5 ingredients; mix well. Spread muffins lightly with butter; spread egg mixture on each muffin half; sprinkle with bacon and cheese. Broil 6 inches from heat until cheese melts, about 3-5 minutes Serve open-faced, and enjoy!
Serves 6-8.

RARE COLLECTION COOKBOOK, The Junior League of Galveston County, Texas

RARE COLLECTION, now in its fourth printing (in five years), is indeed a gem of a cookbook! It guarantees the chef, who prepares and serves any of the cookbook's superb recipes, very immediate compliments from those served! Proceeds from the sale of RARE COLLECTION go to support projects for the community sponsored by the Junior League. Current projects include the Ronald McDonald House and Community Assistance Fund.

JALAPENO STUFFED HAMBURGERS

1 1/2 lbs. ground sirloin
Salt & pepper
1/2 tsp. lemon juice

1 tsp. tarragon leaves
1 tsp. Dijon mustard
2 Tbsps. jalapenos, chopped

2 thick slices Cheddar cheese
2 hamburger buns, heated

Season meat with salt, pepper, and juice. Add tarragon and mustard; mix. Divide meat into 4 equal portions; flatten; place 1 tablespoon jalapenos on 2 of the patties. Top with cheese; cover each with 1 remaining patty. Press edges tightly to seal; oven broil or grill. Serve inside bun.
Serves 2.

Mrs. Fletcher Rabb, Abilene, Texas

WELL WORTH THE HEARTBURN SANDWICH

1 lb. mild sausage, casing
   removed & sliced
1/2 lb. ground beef
1 cup onion, chopped
1/2 cup green pepper,
   chopped

1 (2.5 oz.) can mushrooms,
   sliced & drained
1 (6 oz.) can tomato paste
1 (8 oz.) can tomato sauce
1/4 cup water
1/4 tsp. garlic salt

1/4 tsp. oregano leaves, crushed
1/4 tsp. rosemary, crushed
1/4 cup Parmesan cheese, grated
6 ozs. Mozzarella cheese, grated
1 loaf Vienna (round) bread

In saucepan, brown sausage and beef; drain. Stir in next 3 ingredients; cook 5 minutes. Stir in next 7 ingredients; simmer 10 minutes; stir constantly. Cut top off bread; hollow bread out to form shell. Spread 3 ounces Mozzarella in bottom of bread. Pour meat over cheese; top with rest of cheese. Cover with top of bread; wrap in foil. Bake at 400° until well heated, about 6-8 minutes. Cut into 8 pie shaped sandwiches.

WEST TEXAS HOT SANDWICH

4-6 Tbsps. butter
3-4 Tbsps. flour
Salt & cayenne pepper to taste
2-3 cups milk
2 egg yolks

Tabasco to taste
1 1/2 cups mild Cheddar
   cheese, grated
1/2 cup Parmesan cheese, grated
8 slices bread, trimmed & toasted

4-5 cups chicken, poached &
   sliced
8 slices bacon, slightly cooked
8 slices tomatoes

In saucepan over low heat, melt butter; add next 2 ingredients; stir constantly until smooth. Remove from heat; add enough milk to make smooth cream sauce. Cook over low heat until sauce thickens. Beat in yolks and Tabasco. Stir in cheeses until melted. Put toast in baking dish; cover with chicken; cover completely with sauce; top sauce with 1 slice each bacon and tomato. Broil until bacon is well cooked and sauce slightly browned. A Winner!
Serves 6-8.

THE WILD, WILD WEST COOKBOOK, The Junior League of Odessa, Texas

Published in the Summer of 1991, THE WILD, WILD, WEST COOKBOOK is filled with excellent, new, kitchen-tested recipes that reflect the flair and flavor of living in Odessa and West Texas! Proceeds from the sale of the cookbook are returned to the community. We are happy to be sharing some of these brand new recipes with you!

BREADS

AMIGO BANANA 'N JAM BREAD

1 stick butter, softened
1 cup sugar
2 eggs
1 cup bananas, mashed
1 tsp. vanilla

1 tsp. lemon juice
2 cups flour
1 Tbsp. baking powder
Pinch of salt

1/2 cup raspberry or
    strawberry jam
1 cup pecans or walnuts,
    chopped

Cream butter and sugar; beat until fluffy. Add eggs, one at a time; beat after each addition. Combine next 3 ingredients; stir into egg mixture. Mix well next 3 ingredients; add to bananas; stir to moisten. Fold in jam and nuts. Pour into 2 greased and floured loaf pans. Bake at 350° for 45-50 minutes or tester inserted comes out clean. Cool; turn on rack to remove from pan. **Different and Good!**

Yields 2 loaves.

CRANBERRY BANANA BREAD

1 cup butter, softened
2 cups sugar
2 tsps. vanilla
1 Tbsp. lemon juice
4 eggs

5 very ripe bananas, mashed
3 1/2 cups flour, sifted
1 tsp. salt
2 tsps. baking soda
2 tsps. baking powder

1 cup sour cream
1-2 cups cranberries, cleaned
    & stemmed
1/2 cup nuts, chopped

In bowl, cream butter and sugar; add next 3 ingredients; stir in bananas. Separately, combine flour and next 3 ingredients; stir into banana mixture; mix in rest of ingredients. Pour into 2 greased loaf pans; bake at 350° for 1 1/4 hours or tests done.

Makes 2 loaves.

Ginger Carlin, Dallas, Texas

TEXAS FACT:
Texas was an independent country from March 2, 1836, until December 29, 1845. During that time, the Republic of Texas had four Presidents. They were David G. Burnett, Sam Houston, M.B. Lamar, and Anson Jones.

LEMON BREAD

1 cup sugar	*1½ cups flour*	*1 tsp. vanilla*
½ cup shortening	*1 tsp. baking powder*	*¼ cup sugar*
Rind of 1 lemon, grated	*¼ cup milk*	*Juice of 1 lemon*
2 eggs, slightly beaten	*¼ cup lemon juice*	

Cream sugar and shortening; add rind and eggs; blend well. Sift together flour and baking powder; add alternately with milk and juice to egg mixture; mix after each addition; mix in vanilla. Bake at 350° for an hour. To make glaze, combine rest of ingredients; while loaf is very hot, spoon glaze over top. Enjoy!

Makes 1 loaf. (Freezes well)

Susan Leahy, McAllen, Texas

MAÑANA CHRISTMAS BREAD

1 stick butter	*1½ tsps. baking powder*	*16 ozs. mincemeat*
¾ cup sugar	*½ tsp. baking soda*	*1 cup pecans, chopped*
2 eggs	*¼ tsp. salt*	
2½ cups flour	*½ cup milk*	

Cream butter and sugar; add eggs one at a time; beat after each addition. Combine next 4 ingredients; add to egg mixture, alternating with milk; stir after each addition. Gently stir in mincemeat and nuts. Pour into greased loaf pan; bake at 350° for 1 hour or tests done with cake tester. Bread can be made ahead and frozen until needed mañana! Makes a Super Christmas Gift Wrapped in Plastic Wrap and Tied with a Christmas Ribbon!!

Makes 1 loaf.

Beverly Howell, Bryan, Texas

TEXAS PLACE:
The Santa Ana National Wildlife Refuge near McAllen is home to more endangered species of birds than any other refuge in the United States! With year round temperatures of 70° or more, over 350 species of birds, including the gray hawk, green jay, hook-billed kite, and kiskadee flycatchers, can be found there!

MARVELOUS FOUR IN ONE BREAD

1 large yellow onion, chopped
3 Tbsps. butter
1 egg, beaten
½ cup milk

1½ cups Bisquick
1-1½ cups Cheddar cheese, grated
1 Tbsp. poppy seeds

6 slices bacon, fried crisp & crumbled
1-2 Tbsps. butter, melted

Saute onion in butter until softened. Combine egg and milk; add Bisquick; mix well. Add onion and half of cheese. In greased 8-inch cake pan, spread dough to edges. Top with poppy seeds, bacon, and rest of cheese. Pour butter over all. Bake at 400° for 25-30 minutes or tests done.
Yields 1 delicious loaf!

Addie Baker Nold, Arlington, Texas

POPPY SEED BREAD

¾ cup vegetable oil
1⅓ cups sugar
2 eggs, beaten
2 tsps. vanilla
1 Tbsp. butter flavoring
1 tsp. almond extract

1 cup milk
2 Tbsps. poppy seeds
2 cups flour
1 tsp. baking powder
Non-stick vegetable oil spray

ORANGE GLAZE:
¼ cup orange juice
½ tsp. vanilla
½ tsp. butter flavoring
½ tsp. almond extract
1 cup powdered sugar

In bowl, mix first 7 ingredients; stir in next 3 ingredients. Spray two 8x4-inch loaf pans; add batter; bake at 350° for 1 hour or tests done. To make glaze, combine all ingredients well; pour over hot loaves while they are still in loaf pans. Let glaze soak in well before removing from pans. Results are Super!
Makes 2 delectable loaves!

Helen Smith, Fort Worth, Texas

TEXAS FESTIVAL:
The State Fair of Texas, held annually in Dallas for 16 days in October, is without peer in the United States! The Fair attracts more than 3 million annually to the 200-acre Fair Park and features prize livestock and horse shoe performances, traditional fair exhibits, Broadway musicals and other extravaganzas, and a huge midway that showcases the Texas Star, the largest ferris wheel in the Western Hemisphere!

QUICK SODA BREAD

2 cups flour
2 cups whole wheat flour
1 tsp. salt
3 Tbsps. baking powder

1 tsp. baking soda
1/4 cup sugar
1 Tbsp. cumin
1 tsp. cinnamon

1/4 cup butter, room temperature
1 3/4 cups buttermilk

In bowl, mix well first 8 ingredients. Mix in butter until dough is crumbly; stir in buttermilk until dough is fairly smooth. Divide dough into 2 equal parts; put in 2 greased 9-inch cake pans; pat down. With back of knife made an "X" in middle of each loaf. Bake at 375° for 40-45 minutes or until golden brown. Good!
Makes 2 wonderful loaves!

Martha Lou Rugeley, Wichita Falls, Texas

BLENDER BREAD

1 pkg. yeast
3 Tbsps. sugar
1 cup warm water
1-2 tsps. salt

2 Tbsps. shortening
1/4 cup dry powdered milk
1/2 cup flour, unsifted
1/2 cup wheat germ, optional

4 1/2 cups flour
1 cup water

In blender, mix first 3 ingredients. When all dissolved, add next 5 ingredients. Pour 4 1/2 cups flour into large bowl; add blender mixture to bowl. Pour cup water into (unwashed) blender; mix 8-10 seconds; pour into bowl. Stir with spoon until mixed; knead 5-10 minutes; cover; let rise 1 hour. Punch down; let rise 20 minutes more; half dough. Place in 2 greased loaf pans; let rise 45 minutes more. Bake at 400° for 30-35 minutes or cake tester comes out clean. All yeast breads may be mixed in this manner.
Makes 2 medium loaves.

Mrs. Theron Blair, Odessa, Texas

TEXAS BIG:
When in Odessa, a visit to the world's second largest meteor crater is a treat! The crater is the result of a shower of meteorites that plunged to earth about 20,000 years ago.

59

BLUE RIBBON BREAD BY MARTHA

1 pkg. dry yeast	4 Tbsps. vegetable oil	2 cups water, lukewarm
1 tsp. salt	1 egg	6½ cups flour
⅔ cup sugar		

In bowl, mix all ingredients with half of flour. Place bowl in warm place with no drafts; let dough rise 20 minutes. Mix in rest of flour; let rise to double its bulk. Sprinkle board with flour; knead until dough is smooth and elastic, about 8-10 minutes. Divide dough; put in 2 greased loaf pans. Let rise until dough reaches tops of pans. Cook at 350° for 30 minutes or until golden brown.
Makes 2 loaves.

"This is a good recipe for both new and experienced cooks! Remember when kneading to form dough into round ball, fold it toward you, and then, use heels of hands to push dough away with a rolling motion. Then, turn dough a little, and repeat kneading until dough is smooth. To test for 'double in bulk,' press tips of two fingers lightly into dough; if dent stays, bulk is double. This excellent recipe came to me from my mother's-in-law peerless cook, Martha. It is one I return to time and time again!"

Mary Jo Dudley, Wichita Falls, Texas

TEXAS NOTABLE:
Jose Antonio Navarro, a true Texas patriot, was born in San Antonio in 1795. His career spanned 50 years of Texas history, beginning with Mexico's struggle against Spain and ending with Texas' secession from the United States in 1861. In relation to Texas' struggle against the tyranny of Santa Anna, Navarro signed the Declaration of Independence and was an architect of the Republic and (later) State Constitutions of Texas. In 1936, the Texas Centennial Commission honored Navarro and his wife with a joint monument which attests to Navarro's accomplishments for Texas.

AN ORIGINAL CINNAMON YEAST BREAD

2 pkgs. dry yeast, dissolved in
  1/2 cup warm water
2/3 cup sugar
1 Tbsp. salt

1/4 cup shortening
2 1/4 cups warm water
6-7 cups all purpose flour
1/4 cup butter, melted

2/3 cup sugar
2 Tbsps. cinnamon
Butter, softened

Combine yeast with next 4 ingredients and 3 1/2 cups flour; beat until smooth. Mix in enough remaining flour to make dough easy to handle. Turn dough onto lightly floured board; knead 10 minutes; put in greased bowl; cover. Let rise until double in bulk; about an hour. Punch down; divide in half; roll into 18x9-inch rectangles. Brush each generously with butter. Mix next 2 ingredients well; sprinkle over buttered dough. Roll each into loaf; seal ends. Place seam sides down in well greased baking pan. Cover; let rise in warm place until double, about an hour. Bake at 375° for 40-45 minutes; brush with soft butter when done. Very Special!!

Janis Eklund, Hurst, Texas

CACTUS COUNTRY PUMPKIN BREAD

3 cups sugar
1 cup vegetable oil
4 eggs
2 tsps. vanilla

2 1/2 cups canned pumpkin
1 tsp. salt
2 tsps. baking soda
2 tsps. cinnamon

3 cups flour
3/4 cup dates, chopped,
  optional
2 cups pecans, chopped

Grease and flour 4 1-pound coffee cans or 2 large loaf pans. In bowl, mix sugar and oil. Separately, mix well next 3 ingredients. Combine with sugar mixture. Sift together next 4 (dry) ingredients; add to pumpkin mixture, while beating well with electric mixer. Stir in nuts and dates. Bake at 350° for an hour in coffee cans or 1 1/4 hours in loaf pans.
Yields 4 round or 2 large loaves.

"This bread is wonderful with butter and honey! It makes super sandwiches with a cream cheese filling. It is even better after being frozen or kept for a day or two!"

Lanita Zachry, Abilene, Texas

DILLY CASSEROLE BREAD

1 cup cottage cheese, heated to lukewarm
2 Tbsps. sugar
1 Tbsp. instant minced onion
1 Tbsp. butter
2 tsps. dill weed
1 tsp. salt
1 tsp. soda
1 egg
1 pkg. dry yeast, softened in ¼ cup warm water
2¼-2½ cups flour
Melted butter & salt

Combine first 8 ingredients; add softened yeast; add flour a little at a time to form stiff dough; mix well after each addition. Cover; let rise in warm place until light and doubled in size, about 50-60 minutes; stir down dough; turn into greased 8-inch round pan. Let rise 30-40 minutes more. Bake at 350° for 40-50 minutes or until golden brown. Brush with butter; sprinkle with salt. *Makes 1 delectable loaf.*

Sandy Thompson, San Antonio, Texas

PAT LILE'S SALLY LUNN BREAD

¾ cup warm water
3 pkgs. yeast
⅓ cup sugar
2½ cups milk, lukewarm
⅓ cup oil
2¼ tsps. salt
3 eggs, lightly beaten
16 drops yellow food coloring
8 cups flour, sifted

In large bowl, combine first 3 ingredients; stir until dissolved. Let sit until light and bubbly, about 3-5 minutes. Stir in next 5 ingredients; gradually add flour; beat with wooden spoon until smooth, about 100 strokes. Cover; let rise until light, about an hour. Beat down; pour into 3 greased loaf pans or 1 Bundt pan. Let rise again until within 1-inch of top of pans, about 45 minutes. Bake at 350° for 45-50 minutes.

"This easy recipe makes a rich, yellow bread which is a lovely addition to your Thanksgiving and Christmas tables and is very good for cold turkey sandwiches!"

Jeanne Verlenden, GREAT FLAVORS OF TEXAS

TEXAS FACT:
Amazingly, the first history of Texas written in English did not appear until 1831. The book's title was TEXAS, and it was written by Mary Austin Holly, a relative of Stephen Austin. Before 1831, publications concerning Texas history were in Spanish or French!

JUANA'S ROLLS

1 cup milk
1 tsp. salt
1/2 cup sugar
2/3 cup shortening

2 eggs, beaten
1 cup potatoes, cooked & mashed

1 yeast cake, dissolved in 1/2 cup warm water
5-6 cups flour
1/3 cup butter, melted

In saucepan, combine first 4 ingredients; heat until scalded, i.e., thin skin forms over milk. Pour into bowl; cool; add next 3 ingredients; mix well. Beat in flour, a cup at a time, to make stiff dough. On floured surface, knead; put dough into greased bowl; cover; let rise until doubled in size, about 2 hours. Refrigerate 30 minutes; roll out on floured surface to 1/2-inch thickness; cut with 2-inch round cutter; fold dough in half; seal by pressing edge with fingers. Put rolls in greased baking pan; brush with butter; cover; let rise until size doubles. Bake at 400° for 10-15 minutes or until golden brown. May refrigerate dough for up to 6 days.
Makes 4-5 dozen delicious rolls!

Ed Taylor, Austin, Texas

QUICK BUTTERMILK ROLLS

1 cup buttermilk, lukewarm & thick
1/2 tsp. baking soda

1 tsp. sugar
1 tsp. salt
1 cake compressed yeast

3 Tbsps. vegetable oil
2 1/2 cups all purpose flour, sifted

In bowl, mix well first 4 ingredients; crumble yeast into mixture; stir until dissolved. Add oil and flour; mix well; knead. Shape dough into 18 separate rolls; place in greased baking pan; cover; let rise until doubled in size; bake at 400° for 15 minutes or until golden brown. For whole wheat rolls use 1 1/4 cups whole wheat flour and 1 1/4 cups white flour.
Makes 18 rolls. (Freeze well)

RARE COLLECTION COOKBOOK, The Junior League of Galveston County, Texas

TEXAS TREASURES:
Galveston's nostalgic trolley cars connect the beach at the sea wall to the historic Strand Bay area. The replica "1900 vintage" cars glide for 4 1/2 miles along tracks much like those of Galveston's early days.

BEST BEER BISCUITS

1 (6 oz.) pkg. biscuit mix   1/2 cup beer, warm   Flour (for rolling)
1 tsp. sugar

In bowl, put mix and sugar; stir in beer until blended. Put dough on floured surface; roll to 1/2-inch thickness; cut into biscuits. Place on baking sheet; bake at 425° for 10-12 minutes or until slightly brown.
Yields 6 best biscuits! (Easily doubled)

Diane Sullivan, El Paso, Texas

CAMPFIRE SAUSAGE BISCUITS

3 cups all purpose flour   1 pkg. dry yeast, dissolved in   1 lb. mild *or* hot bulk pork
2 Tbsps. sugar   1/4 cup warm water for 5   sausage, browned,
3/4 tsp. baking soda   minutes   crumbled, & drained
1/2 tsp. salt   1 1/4 cups buttermilk   1/2 cup butter, melted
3/4 cup shortening

Mix well first 4 ingredients. With knife, cut in shortening until mixture is mealy. Add yeast to buttermilk; mix well. Add buttermilk to flour mixture; mix well. With hands, work sausage into dough. On floured board, knead dough 4-6 times. Roll dough to 1/2-inch thickness; cut with round 1-inch cookie cutter. Brush tops with butter; place on cookie sheet; bake at 375° for 15-18 minutes or until golden brown. These are Winners! Serve hot with butter and honey. Also super served at brunch!
Yields about 4 dozen biscuits.

Jeanne Verlenden, GREAT FLAVORS OF TEXAS

TEXAS PLACE:
El Paso is the largest city in the United States on the Mexican border and its neighbor Juarez, Mexico's fourth largest city, is Mexico's largest border city! Their combined populations are about 1.5 million. El Paso's superb climate, scenery, and proximity to Mexico make it one of Texas' most popular tourist areas!

CHRISTMAS BISCUITS

2 cups all purpose flour	3 cups bread flour	1 pkg. yeast, dissolved in 4
5 tsps. baking powder	1/2 tsp. baking soda	Tbsps. warm water
1 tsp. salt	1 cup vegetable shortening	Shaved ham
4 Tbsps. sugar	2 cups buttermilk	

Mix well first 6 ingredients; cut in shortening; add buttermilk and yeast; knead lightly. Roll; cut with 2-inch round cutter. Bake 10-12 minutes at 425°. Split; fill with shaved ham. Serve hot on Christmas morning!

Makes 3 dozen wonderful biscuits!

Sue Sims, San Angelo, Texas

LYNN'S LEMON OR ORANGE BISCUITS

1 stick butter, melted	1/2 tsp. lemon <u>or</u> orange peel,	1/2 tsp. nutmeg
3/4 cup sugar	grated	1/8 cup sugar
3-4 Tbsps. lemon <u>or</u> orange juice	2 10-count cans refrigerated biscuits	

In saucepan, combine first 4 ingredients; heat until sugar dissolves; pour into 9x13-inch pan. Quarter biscuits; place each in pan, rolling in mixture to cover. Combine rest of ingredients; sprinkle over biscuits. Bake at 375° for 25 minutes or brown on top. Good!!

Serves 10.

HEARTS AND FLOURS COOKBOOK, The Junior League of Waco, Texas

TEXAS PLACE:
Waco is home to the TEXAS RANGER HALL OF FAME AND MUSEUM AT FORT FISHER which features a replica of the original Texas Ranger fort established in 1837. The museum's displays commemorate the history and heritage of the Texas Rangers. The museum features a famous collection of guns and weapons from the Old West, Indian artifacts and Western Art, and is headquarters for the present day Company F, Texas Rangers!

NICE 'N EASY BISCUITS

| 1 cup self rising flour | 3 Tbsps. mayonnaise | ½ cup milk |

Mix all ingredients well; spoon into greased muffin tins until ¾ full. Bake at 450° for 10 minutes or until golden brown. Easy and Delicious!
Makes 6-8 biscuits.

POSSUM KINGDOM LAKE BISCUITS

| 1 cup vegetable shortening, melted | 2 pkgs. yeast, dissolved in ¼ cup lukewarm water | 1 tsp. baking soda 5 cups flour |
| ½ cup sugar | 2 cups buttermilk | Margarine, melted |

In bowl, mix shortening and sugar; add yeast. Stir in next 3 ingredients; mix until smooth. Put dough in well greased bowl; cover; refrigerate. (Dough will keep in refrigerator several days.) To bake, pinch off bits of dough the size of walnuts; dip in margarine; smooth tops with fingers; place in baking pan. Bake at 350° for 15-20 minutes or until lightly browned.
Yields about 4 dozen best biscuits!

Faye Gilmore, Possum Kingdom Lake, Texas

Fayle Gilmore is not only a wife, mother, grandmother, and one of West Texas' best cooks but also an avid rattlesnake hunter!!

TEXAS PLACES:
Texas began its marvelous State Park System over 60 years ago and now has over 100 parks for the enjoyment of Texans and their guests! One park definitely worth visiting is Possum Kingdom State Park which is located on the southwestern shore of Possum Kingdom Lake, a 17,700 acre reservoir, located in central Texas!

TEXAS FACT:
In 1925, Texas became the second state in the United States to have a woman governor, Miriam Ferguson. Mrs. Ferguson served Texas as governor for 2 terms.

WRANGLER WHEAT BISCUITS

2½ cups whole wheat flour
½ cup all purpose flour
2 tsps. baking powder
¼ tsp. salt

½ tsp. baking soda
¼ cup margarine, softened
1 pkg. dry yeast, dissolved in 2
    tsps. warm water

1 Tbsp. honey
1 cup buttermilk
¼ cup margarine, melted

Combine first 5 ingredients; cut in margarine until mixture is like coarse meal. Add next 3 ingredients; mix well. Turn dough onto floured surface; roll dough to ½-inch thickness; cut into rounds with 2-inch cookie cutter. Put biscuits on greased baking sheet; brush with melted butter; bake at 400° for 12-15 minutes.

Yields 12 delectable biscuits!

Linda Wingarten, Fort Worth, Texas

BEST TEXAS CORN MUFFINS

½ cup yellow cornmeal
½ cup flour
1 Tbsp. sugar
1 tsp. salt

1 tsp. baking powder
1 egg yolk
1 cup heavy cream
4 Tbsps. butter, melted

1 egg white, beaten stiff
Non-stick vegetable spray

In bowl, mix dry ingredients; stir in yolk, cream and butter; gently fold in egg white. Spray muffin tins; spoon batter into tins; bake at 450° for 12-15 minutes or muffins begin to brown. These will melt in your mouth!

Makes 6 muffins. (Easily doubled)

Sherry Ferguson, GREAT FLAVORS OF TEXAS

TEXAS FACT:
The City of Fort Worth is named after General William Jenkins Worth who fought for Texas in the struggle for independence from Mexico.

BLUE CHEESE MUFFINS

2 cups flour	1 Tbsp. baking powder	1 cup milk
2 Tbsps. sugar	1 cup blue cheese, crumbled	¼ cup butter, melted
Pinch of salt	1 egg, beaten	Sugar for sprinkling

Blend well first 5 ingredients. Separately, mix well next 3 ingredients. Stir egg mixture into dry mixture; mix only until well blended. Pour into greased muffin tins; top each with sugar sprinkle; bake at 400° for 20-25 minutes. Delicious served with Strawberry Gazpacho (page 37)! *Yields 12 wonderful muffins!*

Sue Sims, San Angelo, Texas

GREAT FLAVORS' PECAN MUFFINS

3 cups brown sugar	6 eggs	3 cups pecans, chopped
1 cup flour	1½ tsps. vanilla	
Pinch of salt		

In bowl, mix well all ingredients. Pour into greased muffin tins; bake at 350° for 20-25 minutes or until tops are golden brown. That easy! Great on Sunday or Holiday Mornings! *Makes 16 muffins.*

Madeline Danaher, Wichita Falls, Texas

TEXAS TREASURE:
The Rock Art of the Indians of the Concho River Valley survives on the tall bluffs at Paint Rock Ranch which is located about 30 miles east of San Angelo. With stone cliffs for a canvas, Indians — including Comanches and Apaches — created an unmatched collection of diverse rock art. There is no limit to the subject matter painted on these cliffs — some tell stories while others depict happy hunting grounds, running bison, tomahawks, stars, and a myriad of other images pertaining to the lives and beliefs of people who lived about 2000 years ago! These "pictographs" at Painted Rock Ranch are indeed a treasure as a visual history of some aspects of the lives of the Native Americans who created them!

HOT WATER CORNBREAD MUFFINS

1½ cups white corn meal	1 egg, beaten	1 Tbsp. vegetable shortening
1½ cups water, boiling	1 tsp. salt	
1 cup milk	1 tsp. baking powder	

In bowl, mix corn meal and water. Add next 4 ingredients; mix well. Pour ¼-teaspoon shortening into each muffin tin; add batter; bake at 425° for 15 minutes or until golden brown. *Makes 12 excellent muffins!!*

Diane Sullivan, El Paso, Texas

NANCY'S MORNING GLORY MUFFINS

4 cups flour	4 cups carrots, grated	1 cup coconut (angel flake)
2½ cups sugar	1 cup raisins	6 eggs beaten
4 tsps. baking soda	2 apples, peeled, cored,	2 cups corn oil
4 tsps. cinnamon	& grated	4 tsps. vanilla
1 tsp. salt	1 cup pecans, chopped	

Into bowl, sift together first 5 ingredients; to this, add next 5 ingredients; stir. Separately, combine rest of ingredients; mix well. Add egg mixture to flour/fruit mixture; stir until just combined. Spoon mixture into greased muffins tins. Bake at 350° for 15 minutes or until tops of muffins spring back when touched. Cool 5 minutes; turn onto rack to cool completely. *Makes 2 dozen super muffins!*

William P. Clements, Jr., Texas' Forty-first and Forty-third Governor

TEXAS FACT:
The Butterfield Stage Coach Line, which is probably the most famous stage coach line in the United States, operated entirely in the state of Texas! Its beginning point was Colbert's Ferry, in Grayson County, with the last stop in El Paso, a distance of over 700 miles!

TEXAS HEALTHY MUFFINS

1 cup water, boiling
1 cup raisin bran
1¼ cups brown sugar
½ cup shortening
2 eggs
2 cups bran buds <u>or</u> all bran
3 cups flour
2½ tsps. baking soda
½ tsp. salt
2 cups buttermilk
1 cup nuts, chopped, optional

Pour water over raisin bran; cool. Cream sugar and shortening; add rest of ingredients and cooled bran; mix well. Pour into greased muffin tins; bake at 375° for 15-18 minutes. Dough may be stored in an airtight container in refrigerator for up to a month.
Yields 3 dozen muffins. (Easily doubled or halved)

"My family loves these muffins! I was making them before bran became popular!!"

Beverly Smith, San Antonio, Texas

APPLE COFFEE CAKE

2 sticks margarine
2 cups sugar
3 eggs
1 cup orange juice
½ cup milk
3 cups flour, sifted with 4
   tsps. baking powder
1 cup canned, sliced apples
½ cup sugar plus 4 tsps.
   cinnamon

Cream first 3 ingredients until light and fluffy. Add flour to creamed mixture, alternating with juice and milk, add flour to creamed mixture; stir well after each addition. Blend in apples; pour batter into greased 9x13-inch pan; bake at 350° for 45 minutes. Sprinkle with cinnamon mixture while cake is slightly warm. Enjoy!

Mary Lelicia Garza, San Antonio, Texas

TEXAS TREASURE:
Texas has seven "show caves" that are open to the public. Of these, the caverns of Sonora in central Texas have been called "the most beautiful cave in the world!" The exquisite "Butterfly" is the only formation of its kind in the world. Because of the cave's small opening, it's a clean, sterile cave and has more crystal on its walls than any other!

CHRISTMAS MORNING COFFEE CAKE

2 sticks butter	1 tsp. baking powder	1/2 cup pecans, chopped
1 cup sugar	Pinch of salt	Pam
2 eggs	1 (8 oz.) carton sour cream	1/2 cup confectioner's sugar
2 cups flour	1 tsp. almond extract	2 Tbsps. milk
1 tsp. baking soda	1 (8 oz.) can cranberry sauce	1/2 tsp. almond extract

Cream first 3 ingredients. Separately, combine next 4 ingredients; stir into creamed mixture, alternating with sour cream; add extract. Pour 1/2 batter into greased (with Pam) Bundt pan. Over batter, spoon half cranberry sauce and nuts; cover with rest of batter; top with rest of sauce and nuts. Bake at 350° for an hour or tests done with cake tester. Turn cake out on plate. Mix well rest of ingredients; cover top of warm cake. Wonderful Any Morning!!

EASY CARAMEL ROLLS

Butter	1 (3 oz.) pkg. butterscotch	1 stick butter, cut into small
1 cup pecans, chopped	pudding mix	cubes
1 24-count pkg. frozen yeast dinner rolls	3/4 cup brown sugar	

Generously butter a bundt pan. Sprinkle nuts in bottom of pan; place rolls on top of nuts, narrow end down, side by side; do NOT stack. There will be an inner and outer ring. Combine pudding and sugar; sprinkle over rolls. Top with butter cubes. Cover with towel; allow to rise overnight. Bake at 350° for 30-35 minutes. Turn out of pan onto plate; serve warm. The Perfect Coffee Cake!

HEARTS AND FLOURS COOKBOOK, The Junior League of Waco, Texas

TEXAS BIG:
The world's largest collection of the works and memoirs of the nineteenth century English poets, Robert Browning and Elizabeth Barrett Browning, can be found in the Armstrong-Browning Library, located on the campus of Baylor University in Waco!

STICKY BUN DELIGHTS

1 can Pillsbury flaky biscuits
3 Tbsps. butter, melted
½ cup brown sugar

1½ tsps. cinnamon
⅓ cup pecans, chopped
2 Tbsps. dark corn syrup

¼ cup angel flake coconut,
   optional

Third each biscuit; shape each into ball. Combine sugar, cinnamon, and nuts. Dip each ball into butter; roll in sugar mixture. Place in greased 8-inch round pan. Combine remaining butter and sugar mixture (and coconut); spoon over biscuits. Drizzle syrup over all. Bake at 450° for 10-12 minutes. Serve warm, and enjoy!
Serves 4-6. (Easily doubled)

NEW BRAUNFELS COFFEE CAKE

1 (18.5 oz.) box white cake mix
¾ cup vegetable oil
1 (16 oz.) carton sour cream

½ cup sugar
4 eggs
3-4 Tbsps. brown sugar

2-2½ tsps. cinnamon
1 cup pecans, chopped

Combine first 4 ingredients. Add eggs, one at a time; mix after each addition. Separately, combine rest of ingredients. Pour half of batter into ungreased tube pan; sprinkle half sugar mixture over batter; add rest of batter; top with rest of sugar mixture. Bake at 325° for an hour or tests done. Cool in pan 10 minutes before turning onto plate. A Quick, Good, Moist Accompaniment for Coffee!!

Leslie Baenziger, New Braunfels, Texas

TEXAS FESTIVAL:
For over 30 years, New Braunfels has celebrated Wurstfest every October and November. This season for sausage making is a time of much merrymaking in this wonderful German community!

LA HACIENDA TRADITIONAL SOPAIPILLAS

1 cup flour	*⅓ cup water, hot*	*Honey*
2 tsps. baking powder	*Additional flour, if needed*	*Fresh strawberries, peaches,*
1 Tbsp. sugar	*Peanut oil, 5-inches deep in*	*kiwi or your favorite fruit*
1 tsp. salt	*pan & heated to hot*	
1 Tbsp. vegetable shortening	*1-1½ cups powdered sugar*	

In bowl, using hands or pastry blender, combine well first 5 ingredients; be sure shortening is evenly distributed. Add water; stir with fork until has dough consistency; knead 2-3 times. (If dough is dry; add a little more water; if wet, add 1-2 tablespoons flour.) Put dough in plastic bag; let rise for an hour in warm place. On lightly floured surface, roll dough into rectangle ¼-inch thick (If dough doesn't roll easily, cover; let rest a few minutes more; roll again, etc.); fold dough in half; roll to ¼-inch rectangle again. Cut dough into 3x4-inch rectangles. Fry 1-2 at a time, spooning oil over top to promote puffing. Drain on paper towels; dust with sugar; serve warm topped with honey and fruit. Superb!

Makes 6 sopaipillas. (Easily doubled)

Jan Steger, GREAT FLAVORS OF TEXAS

WONDERFUL MINIATURE SOPAIPILLAS

3½ cups cooking oil   *1 can rolled, prepared biscuits*   *1 cup powdered sugar*

Put oil into medium saucepan; heat to hot. Separate biscuits; flatten each into square. Drop each into oil; fry 1-2 at a time until golden brown, 3-4 minutes. Drain; sprinkle with sugar. Enjoy!

Yields 10 marvelous sopaipillas!

Joy Levens, San Antonio, Texas

REAL TEXAS FOLK'S FACT:
Real Texas Folk know that unless your gate is at least 20 miles from your front door, you do not belong to society as constituted in the Lone Star State!

SOUTH TEXAS KOLACHES

2 pkgs. dry yeast	2 cups flour	2/3 cup butter
1/2 cup water, warm	2 eggs, beaten	2 cups flour
1 Tbsp. sugar	1/2 cup sugar	
1 cup milk, scalded & cooled	1 tsp. salt	

Dissolve yeast in water with sugar; stir; let yeast rise to top. Add milk to yeast mixture; add 2 cups flour; stir until like thin cake batter. Cover; let rise 45 minutes; then, add next 4 ingredients. Gradually sift rest of flour into dough; mix, and stir until dough is spongy and not sticky. Cover; let rise until about double, about 1½ hours. See baking instructions under Filling below.

TOPPING

1 cup flour	2/3 stick butter	Additional butter, melted
1 cup sugar		

Combine first 3 ingredients until crumbly.

FILLING

Stewed fruits of your choice, such as apricots, apples, peaches, etc., cooled

Drop dough by tablespoons on floured board. Roll out like tortilla. Put heaping teaspoon of fruit on dough; pinch dough together to seal; put pinched side down on greased baking sheet. Brush with melted butter; sprinkle with topping; let rise 45 minutes. Bake at 350° for 20-25 minutes or until golden brown. When done, brush with melted butter; cool.

Makes about 3 dozen delectable rolls!

"These freeze well after they are cooked. When ready to use, let thaw; then, warm in oven, uncovered, for about 10 minutes."

Jane McGilvary, McAllen, Texas

TEXAS FACT:
On March 15, 1901, after a very heated session of the Texas Legislature, the bluebonnet was declared to be the State Flower of Texas!

GREEN CHILIES CHEESE BREAD

1 loaf French bread, sliced lengthwise

1 (4 oz.) can chopped green chilies, drained

½-1 cup mayonnaise
2 cups Monterey Jack cheese, grated

Arrange bread cut sides up on baking sheet. Cover with chilies. Mix rest of ingredients; spread over chilies. Bake at 350° for 20 minutes or until hot and bubbly. Cut into wedges, serve, and enjoy! Definitely Texas!!
Serves 12.

Jan Michie, Argyle, Texas

AMARILLO HUSH PUPPIES

1 cup all purpose flour
4 tsps. baking powder
1 tsp. salt

1 large onion, chopped
3-4 Tbsps. red bell pepper, chopped, optional

Milk
Hot oil, 3-inches deep for frying

Mix well first 3 ingredients; stir in next 2 ingredients. Mix in enough milk to make paste, but NOT too thick; let mixture settle for 15 minutes. Drop batter by teaspoonfuls into hot oil. Fry until brown.
Makes 2-3 dozen.

Carolyn Graham, Amarillo, Texas

TEXAS BIG:
Amarillo is home to the largest helium processing plant in the world! Most of the world's supply of helium is found within a 250 mile radius of Amarillo.

TEXAS FACT:
The Helium Monument, in Amarillo, is the only monument to an element in the world!

CHEESE 'N CHILIES CORNBREAD

1 cup yellow corn meal
2 tsps. baking powder
½ tsp. salt
2 eggs

1 (8½ oz.) can cream-style corn
1 stick margarine, melted
1 (8 oz.) carton sour cream

1 cup Cheddar cheese, grated
2-3 (4 oz.) cans chopped green chilies, seeded

Combine first 3 ingredients; add next 4 ingredients; mix well. Stir in rest of ingredients. Bake in greased 8-inch square pan at 350° for 45 minutes. Excellent!
Makes 6 servings.

Mickey Herndon, Austin, Texas

HOUSTON HOT BUTTERED CORN FINGERS

4 Tbsps. butter
2 cups Bisquick
Pinch of salt

1 (8½ oz.) can cream-style corn

Flour for rolling out dough

Melt butter in 15½x10½x1-inch baking pan. In bowl, combine next 3 ingredients; stir until have soft dough; put on floured surface; knead 15-20 times by pressing with fingers. Roll into 6x10-inch rectangle. Take floured knife; cut dough into 1x3-inch strips. Roll strips in butter; arrange strips in single layer in pan; bake at 450° for 10-12 minutes. A Treat for All!
Yields 20 yummy corn fingers!

Ellen Tipton, Houston, Texas

TEXAS NOTABLE:
Ashbel Smith has been called the "Father of Texas Medicine" and the Father of the University of Texas. He served in the Texas State Legislature several times and was one of the founders of the Democratic Party in Texas. He had much to do with establishing a great university, the University of Texas, which has its main campus in Austin.

FIRST PLACE FRENCH BREAD

½ cup butter
½ cup mayonnaise
½ cup Cheddar cheese, shredded

¼ cup chives, chopped
1 (6 oz.) can black olives, sliced
½ tsp. garlic salt

½ tsp. black pepper
1 loaf French bread, sliced
*   into 10-12 pieces*

Mix well first 7 ingredients; spread mixture evenly over each slice. Lay slices "spread up" on cookie sheet. Broil only until edges are brown. Great with Grilled Beef, Chicken, and Pork Dishes!

WILD, WILD WEST TOAST

3 ozs. Parmesan cheese,
*   freshly grated*

½ cup mayonnaise
½ tsp. white pepper

24 slices white sandwich bread,
*   crust removed & quartered*

In bowl, combine first 3 ingredients. Spread 2 teaspoons of mixture evenly over each bread slice. Arrange bread on large baking sheet. Bake at 400° for 5-7 minuters, until golden and bubbly. Serve immediately. Great with All Texas Soups!

WILD, WILD WEST COOKBOOK, The Junior League of Odessa, Texas

ONE MORE JALAPENO CORNBREAD

3 cups cornbread mix
2¼ cups milk
½ cup oil
3 eggs, beaten
1 large onion, chopped

2 Tbsps. sugar
1 cup cream-style corn
½ jalapeno, chopped
1½ cups Cheddar cheese,
*   grated*

¼ lb. bacon, cooked &
*   crumbled*
¼ cup pimento, chopped
1-2 cloves garlic, chopped

Mix together well all ingredients. Pour into greased loaf or 9x9-inch square pan; bake at 400° for 35-40 minutes. This Texas Bread Has It All!! (Freezes well)

Laverne Webb, McAllen, Texas

TEXAS TREASURE:
The Los Ebanos Ferry, located 15 miles west of McAllen, is the last hand drawn ferry on the Rio Grande River. It has become a popular tourist stop. The ferry can move 11 cars and 28 people per hour!

SOUTH OF THE BORDER FLOUR TORTILLAS

2 cups flour *½ tsp. salt* *½ cup water, warm*
1 tsp. baking powder *3 Tbsps. vegetable shortening*

In bowl, mix well first 4 ingredients; add water; knead dough until smooth. (If stiff, add a little more water.) Form dough into medium sized balls; let sit 10 minutes. On smooth surface, use a rolling pin to roll out balls; roll on each side to make flat and round. Cook in skillet over medium heat until brown on each side.

Makes a dozen tortillas.

Victoria Guevara, Farmer's Branch, Texas

TEXAS CORN TORTILLAS

2 cups masa harina (fine corn *1½ Tbsps. salt* *Vegetable oil*
* starch)* *1¼ cups water*

Mix together first 2 ingredients; slowly, add water, mixing constantly. Knead dough until can be shaped into a ball. Divide dough, making 8-10 walnut sized balls. One ball at a time, place ball between 2 sheets of waxed paper; flatten, using palms of hands. With rolling pin, continue to flatten; shape each round until it is a thin disc. Using a small amount of oil, grease heavy skillet; heat over medium heat. Add tortillas, one at a time, cook for less than a minute; turn, cook for about 15 seconds. Stack between pieces of waxed paper as finished. The Real Thing!!

Makes 8-10 tortillas. (Freeze well)

Tortillas, the bread of Mexico, are wonderful when fresh and can be kept frozen for several weeks when well wrapped. Masa harina is available in many supermarkets as well as most gourmet and culinary shops!

TEXAS TREASURES:
There are 4 National Forests located in the Piney Woods region of East Texas. These forests cover 655,076 acres, and each has its own name. They are Angelina, Davy Crockett, Sabine, and Sam Houston.

VEGETABLES AND SIDE DISHES

ALL VEGETABLES' HOLLANDAISE SAUCE

2 eggs
½ tsp. salt
1 stick butter, softened
2 Tbsps. lemon juice

Dash of pepper
1 thin onion slice
1 small garlic clove
½ cup water, hot

Vegetable(s) of your
    choice

In blender, combine first 7 ingredients until smooth. Add water gradually; blend until smooth. Put in top of double boiler; cook over medium heat, stirring constantly, for 20 minutes or sauce coats spoon. Serve hot or cold over favorite vegetables. Marvelous!!
Makes 1½ cups. (Easily doubled)

Jane Findling, San Antonio, Texas

ITALIAN ASPARAGUS

1 lb. fresh asparagus, cleaned
1 red onion, thinly sliced
2 Tbsps. celery, chopped
1 large tomato, sliced

Pinch of salt
¼ tsp. pepper
¼ tsp. oregano
Pinch of thyme

¼ cup Italian bread crumbs
2 Tbsps. Parmesan cheese
3 Tbsps. butter, melted

Line 9x13-inch pan with asparagus; top with onion, celery, and tomato. Sprinkle with seasonings, crumbs, and cheese; drizzle with butter. Cover; bake at 375° for 30-40 minutes or until tender. A REAL TREAT!!
Serves 4 deliciously!!

Gerry Ebner, Wichita Falls, Texas

TEXAS NOTABLE:
Clara Driscoll (1881-1945) was a native of San Antonio, philanthropist, author, rancher, and politician. She believed the Alamo to be the "Greatest Monument in the History of the World!" After 1903, she was known as Savior of the Alamo because she was instrumental in its preservation!

BEST BAKED BEANS

1 lb. ground beef
2 medium onions, chopped
½ stick margarine
¼ cup prepared mustard

3 (15 oz.) cans Ranch Style beans
2 (16 oz.) cans pork & beans

½ cup brown sugar
¼ cup maple syrup
1 cup catsup

Brown beef and onions in margarine; combine with rest of ingredients; refrigerate overnight. Bake at 300° for 1½ hours. For a delicious one dish meal, increase beef to 2 pounds!
Serves 10-12. (Easily doubled)

FLAVORS COOKBOOK, The Junior League of San Antonio, Texas

FRIJOLES MEXICANA
(Mexican Refried Beans)

½ large onion, chopped
¼ cup vegetable oil
2 cups pinto beans, cooked & mashed

1-2 cloves garlic, crushed
¼-½ cup jalapenos, chopped <u>or</u> 1 (4 oz.) can chopped green chilies, drained

1¼ cups Longhorn Cheddar cheese, grated
¼ cup sour cream

Saute onion in oil; stir in next 3 ingredients, ¾ cup cheese, and sour cream. Fry beans over low heat for 10 minutes. Serve hot, topped with rest of cheese. Wonderful! Also Good as a Dip with Chips!
Serves 6-8. (Easily doubled)

Susan Feagan and Demetra Pender, Abilene, Texas

TEXAS PLACES AND FESTIVAL:
Along with the Alamo, there are 4 other Spanish missions in San Antonio. They were all established by Franciscan friars in the early 18th century. They are the Mission Concepcion, Mission de la Espada, Mission San Jose, and Mission San Juan. El Dia de Las Misiones (The Day of the Missions) is a colorful, annual salute to these historic missions on the first Sunday in August.

FRESH BLACK-EYED PEAS

3 cups fresh black-eyed peas,
    shelled
4 cups water

1 tsp. salt
1 Tbsp. sugar
2 small onions, chopped

2 strips bacon, chopped or 2
    tsps. bacon drippings

In saucepan, combine all ingredients; bring to rapid boil. Reduce heat to low; cook for 40 minutes. Wonderful Topped with Texas' Best Chili Sauce (page 100), Chow Chow, or Your Favorite Pickle Relish!
Serves 6.

Virginia Sides, SIDES PEA FARM, Canton, Texas

Virginia has been growing and selling black-eyed peas from her East Texas farm for over 25 years!

MARVELOUS BROCCOLI PIE

2 (10 oz.) pkgs. frozen chopped
    broccoli, cooked & drained
2 cloves garlic, minced
2 Tbsps. vegetable oil

1 lb. Mozzarella cheese, grated
2 ozs. salami or pepperoni,
    finely chopped
1 egg, beaten

1/2 tsp. salt
1/4 tsp. pepper
2 9-inch pastry shells

Saute broccoli and garlic in oil; mix with next 5 ingredients; pour into pastry shell. Top with second shell; deal crust edges together; make "B" on top crust with knife. Put on baking sheet; bake at 350° for 50-60 minutes or until crust is golden. May Be An Appetizer Too!!

FLAVORS COOKBOOK, The Junior League of San Antonio, Texas

TEXAS PLACE:
The City of Canton is noted for First Monday Trade Days which are held the first Monday of each month (and the preceding Friday, Saturday, and Sunday). It features 100 acres of antiques and handmade articles at one of the nation's largest, best known, and most interesting flea markets! Canton is also the home of Brewer's Bells Museum which contains some 3,200 bells, many that are rare and exotic, and the Toy Museum which features a growing display of toy favorites of yesteryear!

BEST COMPANY CARROTS

| 1 stick butter, melted | 1 lb. carrots, peeled & sliced | 1 bunch green onions & tops, chopped |

In saucepan with butter, cook over very low heat, covered, carrots and onions for an hour. Do NOT add water.

Serves 6 deliciously!!

FLAVORS COOKBOOK, The Junior League of San Antonio, Texas

EAST TEXAS SAUTEED GREENS WITH CABBAGE

| 3/4 lb. collard greens, rinsed, stemmed, & coarsely shredded | 2 qts. water, boiling 1 lb. cabbage, coarsely shredded 1/4 cup olive oil | 1 clove garlic, minced 1 onion, thinly sliced Salt & pepper to taste |

Add greens to water; return to boil; cook 3-4 minutes or until greens are tender crisp. Remove greens; leave water in pan. Drain greens in colander. Add cabbage to "greens" water; bring to boil; cook a minute. Drain. In skillet, heat oil over medium low heat; saute garlic and onion 3-4 minutes. Add greens and cabbage; saute 2-3 minutes; season to taste. Marvelous New Way To Enjoy Greens and Cabbage!

Serves 6.   Carolyn Russell, Longview, Texas

TEXAS NOTABLE:
Longview was home to R. G. Tourneau founder of Le Tourneau College. He was the genius responsible for the invention of much of the earth-moving equipment that is used today. The R. G. Le Tourneau Museum, located in Longview, houses his early earth-moving inventions along with interesting information about the man and his life.

TEXAS FACT:
Two famous frontiersmen, Davy Crockett and James Bowie, neither from Texas, believed in the rightness of Texas' struggle for independence from Mexico and gave up their lives for this cause. They both died at the Alamo on March 6, 1836.

CABBAGE PATCH CASSEROLE

1 head cabbage, chopped	¾ cup celery, chopped	2 cups half & half
1 qt. water, boiling	2 Tbsps. butter	1 cup bread crumbs, toasted
¾ cup bell pepper, chopped	1 cup Cheddar cheese, grated	

Boil cabbage in water 5 minutes; drain. Saute bell pepper and celery in butter; add to cabbage along with cheese and half and half; put into 1-quart casserole; top with crumbs. Bake, uncovered, 30 minutes at 350°. Wonderful with Beef and Pork!
Serves 6.

Melinda Galloway, Abilene, Texas

SWEET AND SOUR CABBAGE

1-2 lbs. red cabbage, thinly sliced	3 Tbsps. butter	1½ tsps. flour
¾ cup water	¼ cup brown sugar, firmly packed	1 tsp. salt
3 apples, peeled, pared, & thinly sliced	¼ cup vinegar	Pepper to taste

In large saucepan over medium heat, simmer cabbage in water for 10 minutes; add apples; cook until tender, about 10 minutes. Add rest of ingredients; heat thoroughly. Wonderful with Brisket and Grilled Meats!
Serves 8-10.

Sherry Ferguson, GREAT FLAVORS OF TEXAS

TEXAS FACT:
The City of Abilene was founded in 1881 by Texas cattlemen to be the main livestock shipping place located on the Texas and Pacific Railroad. It was named for Abilene, Kansas, which had been the ending point of the Old Chisholm Trail.

CORNBREAD PUDDING

1 (17 oz.) can creamed corn
1 (17 oz.) can whole kernel
   corn, drained
1 (6 oz.) pkg. cornbread mix
1 cup sour cream
2 eggs, beaten
1 stick butter, melted
2 cups cheese, grated

Mix well first 6 ingredients. Pour into 9x13-inch baking dish; bake at 400° for 20 minutes; reduce heat to 350°; sprinkle cheese on top; bake for 20 minutes more or until completely set and bubbly.
Serves 6-8.

Janie Means, Dallas, Texas

JALAPENO 'N CORN CASSEROLE

2 (3 oz.) pkgs. cream cheese,
   softened
1 stick butter, softened
1/4 cup milk
Dash of garlic salt
2 (11 oz.) cans shoe-peg corn,
   drained
1-3 jalapeno peppers, finely
   minced
Paprika for garnish

In saucepan over low heat, melt and combine first 3 ingredients; mix. Add next 3 ingredients; mix well. Pour into well greased 1½-quart casserole; top with generous amount of paprika; bake at 350° for 20 minutes or until bubbly. Delicious!
Serves 8.

Ken Ridgway, Austin, Texas

MINNIE'S CORN FRITTERS

1 (15 oz.) can whole kernel
   corn, drained *or* 1½ cups
   fresh
2 tsps. baking powder
2 cups flour
1 cup milk
3 Tbsps. sugar
1 Tbsp. margarine, melted
Oil for frying

In bowl, mix first 6 ingredients; beat well. In deep fat fryer, heat oil to 375°; drop batter by spoonfuls into oil; fry for 2-3 minutes or until golden brown. THE BEST!!
Serves 12.

Minnie Bladen, Dallas, Texas

REAL TEXAS FOLK'S FACT:
Texas is so big that the people in Brownsville call the people in Dallas Yankees!

DELICIOUS GREEN PEAS AND BACON CASSEROLE

2 (8 oz.) pkgs. frozen peas,
*   cooked per pkg.'s directions*
3 slices bacon, cut into small
*   pieces*

1 medium onion, chopped
1½ Tbsps. butter
1½ Tbsps. flour
1 cup sour cream

1 (4 oz.) jar whole
*   mushrooms, liquid reserved*

Fry bacon; add onion; saute until onion is clear. Add butter; stir in flour; blend in sour cream
and mushroom liquid. Cook until thick; add mushrooms and peas; gently stir. Heat through.
Enjoy! Different and Good!
Serves 6. (Easily doubled)

Ann Knoebel, San Antonio, Texas

NANCY'S GREEN VEGETABLE CASSEROLE

1 (10 oz.) pkg. frozen baby lima
*   beans, thawed & drained*
1 (10 oz.) pkg. frozen French
*   style green beans, thawed*
*   & drained*

1 (10 oz.) pkg. frozen baby
*   green peas, thawed &*
*   drained*
2 green peppers, seeded, cut in
*   very thin strips, & blanched**

1 cup heavy cream, whipped
1 cup mayonnaise
1 cup Parmesan cheese
Salt & pepper to taste

In greased 2-quart casserole, layer vegetables. Separately, mix together well rest of ingredients;
pour over vegetables. Bake at 350° for 30 minutes or until puffed and brown on top.
Serves 6-8.

Leigh Shamburger, Dallas, Texas

**To blanch, pour boiling water over peppers; drain; rinse with cold water. The purpose of
blanching is to brighten or to remove skins from a specific food.*

TEXAS BIG:
*The world's largest wholesale merchandise market is the DALLAS MARKET CENTER with almost 9.3
million square feet in 8 buildings. The complex covers 150 acres and is host to about 600,000 buyers
annually!*

EGGPLANT AND MOZZARELLA CASSEROLE

1 large eggplant, sliced into rounds	Salt Olive oil	1 lb. Mozzarella, sliced 1 cup tomato sauce

Sprinkle eggplant slices with salt; brush with oil. Place eggplant on baking sheet; broil until brown on both sides. Make "sandwiches" by placing a slice of Mozzarella between 2 slices of eggplant. Bake at 350° until cheese begins to melt. Heat tomato sauce; before serving drizzle over eggplant. A Wonderful Way to use Fresh Mozzarella!!

Serves 6-8. Paula Lambert, Dallas, Texas

EGGPLANT AND MUSHROOM CASSEROLE

3 medium eggplant, peeled	1 cup mayonnaise	3 Tbsps. Gruyere cheese, grated
1 tsp. salt	1 lb. fresh mushrooms, washed, dried, & chopped	1/4 cup fine white bread crumbs
1 cup onion, finely chopped	4 Tbsps. butter	2 Tbsps. butter, melted
2 Tbsps. butter	4 ozs. cream cheese, softened	White mushrooms, thinly sliced
4 eggs, beaten	1/4 cup parsley, finely chopped	
2 tsps. salt	Pinch of thyme	
1/4 tsp. white pepper		

Cover eggplant with water and teaspoon salt; soak 30 minutes; drain; dice. In saucepan, cook eggplant in water until tender; drain. Saute onion in 2 tablespoons butter until golden. In bowl, mix together onion and eggplant; add next 4 ingredients. Separately, saute mushrooms in 4 tablespoons butter; add to eggplant; mix well. Put in 2-quart casserole. Mix cream cheese with next 4 ingredients; sprinkle over eggplant; drizzle melted butter over all. Bake at 350° until set, and top is brown, about 40 minutes. Before serving, top with mushroom slices.

Serves 8-10.

"This excellent recipe comes from Helen Corbitt who prepared it for her private men's cooking class. I believe it to be previously unpublished."

Jim Augur, Dallas, Texas

MUSHROOM AND BARLEY CASSEROLE

1 cup barley	1 (1⅜ oz.) Lipton Onion Soup	1 cup fresh mushrooms,
¼ cup butter,	Mix	sliced
melted	2⅔ cups water	2 Tbsps. butter

In skillet over medium heat, saute barley in butter until barley is golden; stir constantly. Stir in soup mix and water; pour into greased 1½-quart casserole. Bake, uncovered, at 350° for an hour or until liquid is absorbed. Separately, saute mushrooms in remaining butter until tender, about 3-4 minutes. After barley has cooked 1 hour, add mushrooms; stir; bake 15 minutes more. Good, Easy, and Different!

Serves 6.

Gerry Edner, Wichita Falls, Texas

REAL SOUTHERN ONION PIE

3 cups onion, chopped	1 cup heavy cream	2 9-inch pastry shells,
2 sticks butter, melted	Cayenne pepper to taste	uncooked
3 egg yolks, beaten	¾ cup white wine	1¾ cups mild Cheddar
Pinch of salt	3 egg whites, stiffly beaten	cheese, grated

Saute onions in butter until golden; cool. To onions, add yolks and next 4 ingredients; fold in egg whites. Sprinkle half of cheese in each pie shell. Pour half onion mixture over cheese. Bake at 350° for 30-40 minutes or until tester/fork inserted comes out clean. Good Hot or Cold! Super with Beef Dishes!

Serves 12-14.

Nancy Young, Texarkana, Texas

TEXAS FACT:
The City of Texarkana is located on the state line that divides Texas and Arkansas. Thus, half of Texarkana is in Texas and the other half is in Arkansas. The two Texarkanas have separate city governments but share the same Federal Building and Post Office, which was built squarely on the Texas-Arkansas state line! Texarkana is the only city in the United States that has a bi-state Federal Justice (Court and Chambers) Center!

CRAB STUFFED BAKED POTATOES

*2 large russet potatoes, baked
    an hour at 400°*
½ stick butter, melted

¼ cup heavy cream
4 tsps. onion, grated
1 tsp. salt

4 ozs. Cheddar cheese, grated
*1 cup crab meat, fresh or
    canned, rinsed*

Split potatoes in half lengthwise; scoop out pulp; reserve shells. In bowl, mash pulp; add next 5 ingredients. Gently, fold in crab meat; fill shells with potato/crab mixture; place on baking sheet. Bake at 450° for 15 minutes or until bubbly. A Real Treat!
Serves 4.

FIESTA STUFFED BAKED POTATOES

*6 large baking potatoes,
    baked an hour at 400°*
*3 medium ripe avocados,
    peeled & mashed*
6 Tbsps. picante sauce

1½ tsps. cilantro or parsley
Salt & pepper to taste
Garlic powder to taste
*¾ cup Monterey Jack cheese,
    grated*

*¾ cup mild Cheddar cheese,
    grated*
*Cilantro or parsley for
    garnish*

Slice thin layer off tops of potatoes; scoop out pulp; put in bowl; mash. Separately, mix avocados with next 4 ingredients; add this to mashed potatoes; mix well. Spoon mixture into potato shells; place in glass baking dish. Combine cheeses; sprinkle on top of each; bake at 300° for 10-15 minutes or until cheese melts.
Serves 6.

"This is a recipe my husband, Michael, created. They were first served to our children who are hard to please, and they loved them!"

Carolann Gerescher, San Antonio, Texas

TEXAS FACT:
Plainview is the county seat of Hale County which is one of the top ten vegetable producing counties in Texas. Presently, more than 450,000 acres are under cultivation! Hale County is located in the High Plains region of Texas in the heart of the Panhandle.

VERY BEST HASH BROWN POTATOES

1 (32 oz.) pkg. hash brown frozen potatoes, thawed
1 onion, chopped & sauteed in 1 Tbsp. margarine
1 (8 oz.) carton sour cream
1 (10¾ oz.) can cream of celery soup
1 (10¾ oz.) can cream of mushroom soup
1 stick margarine, melted
12 ozs. mild Cheddar cheese, grated
2 cups corn flakes, crushed
½ stick margarine, melted

Mix well first 7 ingredients. Spread in greased 9x13x2-inch baking dish. Combine rest of ingredients; spread over potatoes. Cover; refrigerate overnight. Bake, uncovered, at 350° for an hour; top will be bubbly.

Serves 12-15.

"I've never served this casserole to anyone who didn't love it!"

Jane Pool, Pipe Creek, Texas

CRUNCHY SWEET POTATO CASSEROLE

3 cups sweet potatoes, cooked & mashed
1 stick margarine, melted
1 (5 oz.) can evaporated milk
1 cup sugar
2 eggs, beaten
1 tsp. vanilla
½ tsp. nutmeg
1 tsp. cinnamon
½ cup pecans, chopped
1 cup corn flakes, slightly crushed
½ cup brown sugar, firmly packed
1 stick margarine, melted

Mix well first 8 ingredients; pour into 9x13-inch baking dish. Combine rest of ingredients; spread evenly over potatoes. Bake at 350° for 30 minutes or until top is golden brown. A Super Holiday Treat!

Serves 8.

Carolyn Colquitt, Dallas, Texas

TEXAS FACT:
Dotted throughout the City of Dallas are 271 parks covering more than 20,000 acres including the wonderful Elm Fork Nature Trail!

GREEN CHILIES 'N RICE CASSEROLE

1 (4 oz.) can chopped green
  chilies, drained
2 cups sour cream
1 tsp. salt

3 cups rice, cooked
8 ozs. Monterey Jack cheese,
  grated

⅛ tsp. pepper
2 Tbsps. butter

Mix well first 3 ingredients; set aside. Put 1 cup rice in greased 1½-quart casserole; spoon ⅓ of chilies mixture and ⅓ cheese over rice. Repeat layering twice. Sprinkle with pepper; dot with butter. Cover; bake at 350° for 20 minutes; uncover; bake 10 minutes more. Do not overcook! May be frozen unbaked. Texas Staple That's Good with a Texas-sized Steak!!
Serves 6. (Easily doubled)

Martha Ferguson, Abilene, Texas

TEXAS RICE

¼ cup margarine, melted
1 cup green onions & tops,
  chopped
4 cups rice, cooked

2 cups sour cream
1 cup cottage cheese
2 (4 oz.) cans chopped green
  chilies, drained

2 cups Cheddar cheese, grated
Dash of salt & pepper
Paprika & fresh parsley for
  garnish

Saute onion in margarine until tender. Combine rice with onions and next 5 ingredients; mix well. Bake, uncovered, at 375° for 30 minutes or until hot and bubbly. Sprinkle with garnishes. Delicious!
Serves 8.

"This is very good with Mexican food or with baked ham!"

Mikey Herndon, Austin, Texas

TEXAS FACT:
In 1907, C.W. Post, the famous cereal manufacturer, founded the town of Post, Texas, which is located in the Panhandle.

RICE AND APRICOT PECAN STUFFING FOR WILD GAME

1 cup rice, uncooked
1 cup water
1 cup chicken broth
1 Tbsp. butter
½ tsp. salt
¼ tsp. coarse black pepper
1 stick butter, melted
1 cup onion, chopped
½ cup mushrooms, sliced
1 cup apricots, minced
½ cup pecans, chopped
& toasted

In saucepan over low heat, cook rice with next 5 ingredients until all liquid is absorbed. In skillet, saute onions in butter until golden. Add mushrooms and apricots to onions; cook until tender. Add vegetable mixture and pecans to rice. Serve immediately. Delicious with Wild Turkey and other Game Fowl!!

Serves 8.   Susan Teeple Auler, Austin, Texas

Susan started the HILL COUNTRY FOOD AND WINE FESTIVAL and owns FALL CREEK VINEYARDS!!

WINNER FRITO CORN DRESSING

1 (12 oz.) bag Fritos, crumbled
1 (17 oz.) can cream-style corn
1 cup milk
2 slices bread
2 eggs
1 large onion, chopped
1 large green pepper, chopped
Leaves of 6 celery stalks
2 Tbsps. oil

Put Fritos in bowl; cover with next 4 ingredients; set aside. Saute remaining ingredients in oil until tender. Combine with Frito mixture; mash just enough to coarsely blend all ingredients. Pour in greased 2-quart casserole; bake at 350° for 50-60 minutes. Excellent!
Serves 8. (Easily doubled. Freezes well.)

"My mother created this recipe when Fritos first appeared on the market. It is a definite original and is delicious with or without the turkey!!

                                                              Hilda Lewin, McAllen, Texas

TEXAS PLACE:
The Fall Creek Vineyards, nestled in Texas Hill Country on the shores of Lake Buchanan, is open to the public every Saturday afternoon from January through October.

CALICO COUNTY'S BAKED SQUASH

*2½ lbs. yellow squash,
cleaned & cut into 1-inch
thick slices*
3 Tbsps. margarine

1 egg, beaten
1 Tbsp. sugar
½ tsp. salt
1 tsp. pepper

1 small onion, finely chopped
1 cup cornbread crumbs
½ cup Cheddar cheese, grated

Put squash in saucepan; cover with water; cook until tender. Drain; add next 7 ingredients; mix thoroughly. Place mixture in greased casserole dish, and sprinkle with cheese. Bake for 20-25 minutes at 350°.

Makes 4 marvelous servings!

Bob LaRoche, CALICO COUNTY RESTAURANT, Amarillo, Texas

DELICIOUS SQUASH 'N BLUEBERRY CASSEROLE

*4 acorn squash, halved &
seeded*
*12 ozs. fresh or frozen
blueberries*

*1 apple, peeled, pared,
& finely diced*
8 Tbsps. brown sugar

8 tsps. butter

Place squash in baking dish, cut side up. Sprinkle berries and apple in cavity of each squash. Top each with 1 tablespoon sugar and 1 teaspoon butter. Cover; bake at 350° for 30-35 minutes. Super with Wild Game, Turkey, and Chicken Dishes!

Serves 8.

Susan Bagwell, Dallas, Texas

TEXAS BIG:
Amarillo is home to the American Quarter Horse Association. The Association has the world's largest equine registry, more than 1.2 million horses registered in 53 countries! The Quarter-Horse was the first American horse breed and is still the favorite mount of cowboys!

RIO GRANDE SQUASH

5-8 yellow squash, peeled &
   sliced in rounds
3 Tbsps. instant minced onion
4 Tbsps. butter

1-1½ cups Cheddar cheese,
   grated
1 (10 oz.) can Ro-Tel tomatoes
   & green chilies

Salt & pepper to taste
2 Tbsps. butter, melted
Ritz cracker crumbs

In skillet, cook squash with onion until tender; drain. In 2-quart casserole, combine squash with next 4 ingredients; stir well. Drizzle melted butter over all; top with crumbs. Bake at 350° for 30 minutes or until hot and bubbly. Add a pound of cooked ground chuck for a tasty main dish!

Serves 6-8.   **Sandy Thompson, McAllen, Texas**

FRESH ZUCCHINI WITH CARROTS CASSEROLE

1 cup water, boiling
4 medium zucchini, washed
   & sliced
1 tsp. salt
4 Tbsps. butter, melted
1¾ cups carrots, grated

1 medium onion, grated
½ cup mayonnaise
1 (10¾ oz.) can cream of
   chicken soup
Dash of garlic powder
Dash of pepper

1 Tbsp. seasoned bread
   crumbs
2 Tbsps. butter, melted
⅓ cup seasoned bread crumbs

In saucepan with water, cook, covered, zucchini and salt until tender, about 10 minutes; drain; set aside. In 4 tablespoons butter, saute carrots and onions until tender. Separately combine mayonnaise with next 3 ingredients; add zucchini, carrots, onions, and a tablespoon bread crumbs. Pour into well greased 2-quart casserole; mix last 2 ingredients; sprinkle over zucchini; bake at 350° for 30-35 minutes.

Serves 6 delectably!

Charlotte Brunette, Wichita Falls, Texas

TEXAS BIG FACTS:
It is 150 miles further from El Paso to Texarkana than it is from Chicago to New York City! Fort Worth is nearer St. Paul, Minnesota, than it is to Brownsville, Texas!!

CHRISTMAS SPINACH

2 (10 oz.) pkgs. frozen
chopped spinach, cooked
per pkg.'s directions &
drained

½ cup mushrooms, sliced
2 Tbsps. onion, grated
2 Tbsps. butter
2 (6 oz.) cans tomato paste

1 cup sour cream
Paprika

Saute mushrooms and onion in butter. Toss spinach with mushroom mixture; put in greased 2-quart casserole; spread tomato paste on top; cover with sour cream. Sprinkle with paprika; bake, uncovered, at 350° for 20 minutes or until heated.
Serves 8.   Shirley Fancher, Amarillo, Texas

JALAPENO SPINACH CASSEROLE

2 (10 oz.) pkgs. frozen
chopped spinach, cooked
per pkg.'s directions &
drained; reserve ½ cup
liquid

½ stick butter, melted
2 Tbsps. onion, chopped
3 Tbsps. flour
½ cup milk
½ tsp. each salt & pepper

¾ tsp. celery salt
¾ tsp. garlic salt
1 tsp. Worcestershire sauce
1 (6 oz.) roll jalapeno cheese
Bread crumbs

Cook onions and flour in butter until onions are soft; add to spinach. Separately, combine reserved liquid with rest of ingredients, except bread crumbs. Cook over medium heat until cheese melts; combine with spinach; pour into 9x13-inch greased casserole. Sprinkle with crumbs; bake at 350° for 20-25 minutes or hot and bubbly.
Serves 6-8.
HEARTS AND FLOURS COOKBOOK, The Junior League of Waco, Texas

TEXAS FESTIVALS:
Six gracious Southern mansions, located in Waco, open their doors for special tours during the Brazos River Festival which is held every year during the third week in April.

Another Waco Festival is the Christmas-on-the-Brazos Celebration which is held annually the first weekend during December.

GRINGO BROILED TOMATO CUPS

5-6 tomatoes, each halved	1/4 cup Parmesan cheese	3 green onions & tops,
1/2 cup sour cream	1 tsp. garlic salt	chopped
1/2 cup mayonnaise	Juice of 1 lemon	

Combine sour cream with next 5 ingredients; spread mixture evenly on top of tomato halves. Arrange in baking dish, broil until bubbly, about 3 minutes; watch closely. Excellent!
Serves 10-12.

MIGAS
(Eggs and Tortillas)

6 Tbsps. bacon drippings	1 small onion, chopped	1/2 tsp. ground cumin
8-10 four tortillas, cut in 1-inch squares	1 large tomato, chopped	Salt to taste
	1 1/2 Tbsps. chili powder	6 eggs, beaten

In skillet, fry tortillas in hot drippings until tortillas begin to brown; stir constantly. Push tortillas to side of pan; drain away some of drippings; add next 5 ingredients; saute until onion is transparent. Mix with tortillas; add eggs; gently stir until eggs are done. Super!
Serves 4-6.

CALICO EGGS

12 eggs	1-2 avocados, chopped	1-2 tomatoes, chopped
3 ozs. cream cheese		

In skillet, scramble eggs over medium heat. When almost done, add cream cheese; stir to heat. Remove from heat; add avocado and tomato.
Serves 6.

"A tasty and easy breakfast dish that is perfect for spur of the moment weekend company!"

HEARTS AND FLOURS COOKBOOK, The Junior League of Waco, Texas

TEXAS FACT:
There is more timberland in East Texas than in all of New England combined!

BEST BRUNCH EGGS

8 eggs, hard-boiled, sliced lengthwise, & yolks removed	¼ tsp. prepared mustard	1 cup milk
½ stick butter, melted	1 tsp. onion, minced	1 (10¾ oz.) can cream of shrimp soup
¼ tsp. salt	¼ tsp. curry powder	½ cup Cheddar cheese, grated
Dash of pepper	2 Tbsps. butter, melted	1 cup bread crumbs, buttered
	2 Tbsps. flour	

In bowl, combine yolks and next 6 ingredients; mash with back of fork; mix well. Spoon into egg whites; place in baking dish yellow side up. In saucepan, stir flour into butter; cook 1-2 minutes. Slowly add milk; cook until thick; stir often. Stir in soup and cheese; cook until cheese melts. Pour over eggs; top with crumbs; bake at 350° for 30-35 minutes.

Serves 8. (Easily doubled)   Shirley Fancher, Amarillo, Texas

BRUNCH OMELET BY BRUCE

8 egg yolks, whisked until frothy	4 Tbsps. butter	Sugar for sprinkling
8 egg whites, beaten until very stiff	1 Tbsp. peanut oil	4 Tbsps. cognac or rum, optional
4 tsps. sugar	3 Tbsps. Cointreau	
	1½ cups bananas, sliced & heated in 2 Tbsps. butter	

Fold yolks into whites; add sugar. In omelet pan, heat butter and oil to very hot; pour in eggs. Spoon Cointreau over eggs; cook until omelet is done but still moist. Put bananas in omelet's center; fold omelet over; put on heated, oven proof plate; top with sugar; glaze under broiler a minute. Add cognac; broil a minute more. Serve immediately. Delightful!

Serves 4-6.   Carolyn Bruce Rose, Dallas, Texas

TEXAS NOTABLE:
Dwight D. Eisenhower was born in Denison, Texas, in 1890. Eisenhower was the 34th President of the United States, serving from 1952-60. Before becoming president, Eisenhower was Commander-In-Chief of the (European) Allied Forces during World War II. From 1948-53, he was President of Columbia University in New York City.

SANTA'S EGGS

1 Tbsp. butter
1 dozen eggs, beaten
1/2 cup milk
Pinch of salt & pepper

1 cup sour cream
12 slices bacon, cooked crisp,
   & crumbled

2 ozs. sharp Cheddar cheese,
   grated
2 ozs. Monterey Jack cheese,
   grated

In skillet over medium low heat, melt butter. Combine next 3 ingredients; pour over butter. Cook until eggs are barely set; cool. Stir in sour cream. Butter 2-quart baking dish; pour in egg mixture; top with bacon and cheeses. Cover; refrigerate overnight. Bake in preheated 300° oven for 20-25 minutes.

Serves 10-12 sumptuously!!

"You may vary this recipe by using green chilies, your favorite cheeses, light sour cream, or yogurt. This dish is super on Christmas morning or for entertaining when you want to prepare brunch in advance."
                                          Sue Sims, San Angelo, Texas

SHARPE'S HOLIDAY EGG SOUFFLE

1 1/2 sticks butter, softened
8 slices white sandwich
   bread, crusts removed

1 lb. sharp Cheddar cheese,
   grated
3 cups milk

1 Tbsp. prepared mustard
6 eggs

Butter sides and bottom of 2-quart baking dish. Spread butter on both sides of bread. Cut bread into 1-inch cubes. Alternate layers of bread and cheese, ending with cheese. Beat together well remaining ingredients; pour over bread and cheese. Cover; refrigerate overnight. Bake at 350°, uncovered, an hour (with foil underneath to catch drippings).

"This souffle is served every Christmas morning in our home."

                                          Margaret Sharpe, Dallas, Texas

TEXAS TREASURES:
Texans are the friendliest people in the world, and Texas women are the most beautiful on this good earth!

ERNESTO'S HOT SAUCE

1 lb. tomatillos, halved
5 serrano chiles, stemmed &
* seeded*
1-2 tsps. sugar
1 clove garlic, finely minced
2 Tbsps. white vinegar
¾ cup cooking oil, heated
Salt to taste

In medium saucepan, bring first 5 ingredients to boil; simmer 8-10 minutes. Transfer mixture to blender; blend until smooth and light, about 2 minutes. Leave blender on; slowly add oil. Season with salt. Sauce may be served hot or cold, and keeps well, refrigerated, for 2 weeks. If necessary, blend again to restore texture. Serve as sauce for grilled or broiled seafood and freshwater fish dishes. Excellent!
Makes about 3 cups.

Ernesto Torres, ERNESTO'S RESTAURANT, San Antonio, Texas

MILD PICANTE SAUCE

2 garlic cloves, chopped
4 serrano peppers, seeded &
* finely chopped*
1 bunch cilantro, stemmed
1 medium onion, finely
* chopped*
1 (28 oz.) can peeled tomatoes
Salt to taste
1 (8 oz.) can tomato sauce

In blender, combine first 4 ingredients. Add remaining ingredients; blend well. Sauce will be a little chunky. Store in quart jar; refrigerate. Keeps for weeks!
Yields 1 quart of Texas Goodness!!

"This sauce is super on everything from fajitas to chalupas to just plain chips as a dip!"

Jane Findling, San Antonio, Texas

TEXAS FACT:
Spanish explorers first saw Texas in 1519 and began their exploration of it almost 100 years before the Pilgrims landed at Plymouth Rock!! From Spanish, and later Mexican rule, Texas acquired much of its unique and rich heritage and, of course, the "Tex-Mex" and Southwestern approach to cooking that has evolved and become such a fine art over time!

SALSA PICANTE
(Hot Sauce)

1-3 jalapenos	½ tsp. salt	1-2 Tbsps. oil from canned
1-2 pods fresh garlic	1 (28 oz.) can peeled	jalapenos
1 (16 oz.) can tomatoes & juice	tomatoes	Ground black pepper

In blender at high speed, mix first 4 ingredients for 35 seconds. Add tomatoes; blend on low speed 2-3 seconds or until has sauce consistency; add oil and pepper. Store in glass jar. Keeps refrigerated for several weeks. Great on huevos rancheros (camp cook's eggs), sandwiches, with cottage cheese, and to spice up stews and soups!
Makes 1 ½ quarts.

TEXAS BEST CHILI SAUCE

4 qts. ripe tomatoes, peeled, cored, & chopped	1 fresh hot red pepper, minced	1 Tbsp. celery seeds
2 cups onion, chopped	1 cup sugar	1 Tbsp. mustard seeds
2 cups sweet red pepper, chopped	3-4 Tbsps. pickling salt	2½ cups vinegar (with
	3-4 Tbsps. mixed pickling spices	5% acidity)

In 10-quart Dutch oven, combine first 6 ingredients; simmer, uncovered, 45 minutes. Tie next 3 ingredients inside a cheesecloth bag; add to tomato mixture. Simmer, uncovered, about 1½ hours or until thickened. Stir in vinegar; simmer an additional hour or until mixture reaches desired thickness; remove spice bag. Pour chili sauce into hot sterilized jars; leave ¼-inch space at top. Cover at once with metal lids; screw bands tight. Boil in water bath for 15 minutes. Delicious with Almost any Meat Dish!!
Yields 4 pints. (Easily doubled or halved)

Amy Levine, Austin, Texas

TEXAS NOTABLE:
Elisabet Ney was a nationally recognized Texas sculptor. Ney, who died in 1907, lived in Austin and created the statues of Stephen Austin and Sam Houston that stand in honor at the Texas State Capitol in Austin. Some of her sculptures can also be seen at the Capitol Building in Washington, D.C.

PICO DE GALLO

1 Tbsp. olive oil
1 cup onion, finely diced
1 clove garlic, minced
1 Tbsp. cilantro, minced
4 firm ripe tomatoes, peeled, seeded, & diced
1 jalapeno, seeded & minced
Salt & pepper to taste

In skillet over medium heat, briefly saute onion and garlic in oil. Add cilantro; let cool; combine with rest of ingredients. Serve at room temperature with chips, meats, etc. Adds Zip To Most Foods!

"This relish is really the Granddaddy of Southwestern Relishes and one of the best!"

Anne Lindsey Greer, Dallas, Texas

TEJAS SALSA

2 tomatillos (Mexican green tomatoes), skin removed
3-5 large garlic cloves
5 medium tomatoes, chopped
1/4 cup fresh cilantro, chopped
1 Tbsp. fresh lemon juice
1 tsp. black pepper
2-3 jalapeno peppers, thinly sliced

In blender, mix first 2 ingredients until pasty smooth. In bowl, combine rest of ingredients; add blender mixture. Cover; refrigerate an hour or overnight to blend flavors. Perks up Mexican and Meat Dishes!
Makes 2 cups. (Easily doubled)

REAL IMITATION MEXICAN TAMALES

1 cup Cheddar cheese, grated
1 cup Monterey Jack cheese, grated
6 green onions & tops, chopped
6 (6-inch diameter) flour tortillas (page 78)
6 Tbsps. or to taste Tejas Salsa (above)

Combine cheeses and onions; divide by six; put in center of each tortilla; cover with salsa. Fold bottom of tortilla over filling; fold 2 sides over filling; fold top side over filling (as with envelope). Wrap each tortilla in 8x12-inch piece of foil; heat at 300° for 10-15 minutes or until cheese has melted. Good!
Serves 6. (Easily doubled)

GREEN CHILIES 'N CHEESE PIE

1 9-inch deep dish pastry shell
2½ cups Monterey Jack
  cheese, grated
1 (4 oz.) can chopped green
  chilies

1 cup onion, chopped
2 Tbsps. margarine
4 eggs, lightly beaten
1¼ cups half & half

½ tsp. pepper
Picante sauce
  (page 99)

Bake shell for 5 minutes at 475°. Put half of cheese in shell; top cheese with half the chilies. Repeat layering again. Saute onions in margarine; combine with next 3 ingredients; pour over chilies; bake at 375° for 30-35 minutes or firm. Serve with picante sauce. Excellent!
Serves 6 amply!

TORTILLA TARTA DE VERDURA
(Vegetable Tortilla Pie)

2 yellow onions, chopped
1-2 cloves garlic, crushed
2 (14½ oz.) can stewed
  tomatoes
2-3 stalks celery, chopped

2 (4 oz.) cans chopped green
  chilies
Salt & pepper to taste
12 tortillas, quartered
3 Tbsps. peanut oil

2 lbs. mild Cheddar cheese,
  grated
3 cups sour cream

In skillet, simmer first 6 ingredients for 12-15 minutes. Separately, heat oil to hot; add corn tortillas; heat until softened. Layer in 9x13-inch pan as follows; ⅓ tortillas, ⅓ tomato mixture, ⅓ cheese. Repeat layering twice. Heat at 350° for 15-20 minutes or until cheese is melted and top bubbles. Slice, top with sour cream, and enjoy!
Serves 10.

Jan Steger, **GREAT FLAVORS OF TEXAS**

TEXAS PLACE:
The City of Midland, Texas, lies over what was once (variously) known as the Chihuahua Trail, the Emigrant Road to California, and the Comanche War Trail! Midland was established in 1885 by thrifty midwestern families, and its predominant economic base was agricultural until the 1923 discovery of oil in the Permian Basin. Midland is home to the Museum of the Southwest which is dedicated to the preservation and interpretation of Southwestern Art and Culture as well as the Permian Basin Petroleum Museum, Library, and Hall of Fame which is a popular visitor site!

WONDERFUL VEGETABLE CHALUPA
(A Chalupa Is Tortilla Dough Shaped Into An Oval Or Boat That's Filled With Shredded Meats And Vegetables.)

4 cups onion, chopped	2 cups green onions & tops, chopped	3-4 cups Cheddar cheese, grated
4 cups zucchini, sliced in rounds	8 Tbsps. olive oil	1 large avocado, sliced
3½ cups mushrooms, sliced	10-12 corn tortillas (page 78)	1-2 pts. sour cream
3 cups celery, chopped	5 medium tomatoes, chopped	Picante sauce (page 99)

In large skillet, saute first 5 ingredients in oil until tender crisp, about 15 minutes. Separately, in dry skillet, brown tortillas for about 15 seconds each side. Put each tortilla on oven proof plate; top with sauteed vegetables; add by spoonfuls tomatoes, cheese, and avocado. Broil just until bubbly. Top with dollop of sour cream; serve with picante sauce. 4-5 cups cooked and shredded beef or chicken may be added for a heartier entree!
Serves 10-12 very well!

ZESTY CAULIFLOWER CON QUESO

1 large cauliflower, broken into flowerets & cooked	1 (16 oz.) can tomatoes	¼ tsp. Tabasco sauce
¼ stick butter, melted	1 bay leaf	4 ozs. mild Cheddar cheese, grated
¼ cup onion, chopped	1 tsp. salt	
2 Tbsps. flour	1 (4 oz.) can chopped green chilies, drained	

Cook flowerets until tender crisp; drain. In saucepan, cook onion in butter until tender, about 5 minutes; blend in flour; stir in tomatoes. Cook; stir constantly until mixture thickens and comes to a boil. Add next 4 ingredients; cook 5 minutes; add cheese; stir until melted. Serve hot over flowerets. The sauce is good on other vegetables and meats and is also good over scrambled eggs!
Serves 4-6.

FLAVORS COOKBOOK, The Junior League of San Antonio, Texas

STRAWBERRY BUTTER

1½ cups powdered sugar   *1 stick butter, softened*   *1 tsp. lemon juice*
1 cup fresh strawberries

In blender or food processor, combine all ingredients. Process until berries are chopped. Spread on hot rolls or biscuits. Delicious! Frozen or fresh cranberries can take the place of strawberries. Good!
Makes 1 cup.

HEARTS AND FLOURS COOKBOOK, The Junior League of Waco, Texas

WONDERFUL PEAR BUTTER

6 lbs. pears, peeled, seeded,   *¼ cup lemon juice*   *4 cups brown sugar, firmly*
  & chopped   *2 tsps. cinnamon*   *packed*
1¼ cups water   *½ cup port wine*

In saucepan, combine first 3 ingredients; cook over medium heat for 30 minutes or until pears are soft; take from heat; mash. Add rest of ingredients; cook over low heat an hour or until thickened. Pour into sterilized jars; seal. May substitute apples for pears. A Wonderful Topping for Cooked Cereals, Meats, and Toast!
Makes approximately 6 pints.

David Tiller, Dallas, Texas

REAL TEXAS FOLK'S FACT:
Real Texas Folk know that there is no other state in the United States that can boast major cities as diverse and distinctive as Houston, Austin, Dallas, San Antonio, Fort Worth, Galveston, Corpus Christi, El Paso, and Waco to name just a few!!

FRESH CRANBERRY RELISH

1 navel orange, cut into small pieces
1/2 lime, seeded & cut into small pieces
1/2 cup pitted dates
1 large tart apple, cored & cut into small pieces
1/2 cup sugar
3 cups fresh cranberries, rinsed

In blender, chop orange and lime until finely chopped. Add next 3 ingredients; blend until apples and dates are chopped. Add cranberries; blend until coarsely chopped. Refrigerate; serve cold. Relish keeps for a month in refrigerator! Marvelous Accompaniment To Any Baked Or Roasted Fowl!

Yields 4 1/2 cups.

Amy Levine, Austin, Texas

BRAZOS CAFE MANGO CHILI RELISH

Juice of 1 large lime
3 ripe mangos, peeled & diced
8 ripe peaches, blanched*, peeled, & diced
1/4 tsp. coriander
5 serrano or jalapeno peppers, stemmed & diced
1/4 tsp. ground allspice
1 bunch green onions & tops, finely chopped
1 Tbsp. fresh mint, chopped
2 cloves garlic, finely diced
2 Tbsps. fresh cilantro, chopped
1 Tbsp. fresh chives, chopped
Salt & white pepper to taste
1-1 1/2 ozs. tequila, optional

Cover fruits with juice. Separately, mix well rest of ingredients; gently toss into fruit. Adjust salt and pepper to taste; add more lime juice if desired. Cover; refrigerate at least an hour before serving. Wonderful Accompaniment To Grilled Meats!

Makes 4 cups.

Chef Nancy Beckham, BRAZOS CAFE, Dallas, Texas

*How to blanch, see page 86.

TEXAS FACT:
The Brazos is Texas longest river. It was named Brazos de Dios by Spanish explorers. The name means "Arms of God" and legend has it that the river was so named by Spanish explorers who were dying of thirst when they found the river and hailed it as the answer to their prayers!

WONDERFUL MIXED-UP PICKLES

1 cup pickling salt
4 qts. cold water
4 cups small cucumbers, in 1-inch slices
2 cups carrots, in 1½-inch slices
2 cups onion, chopped
2 cups celery, in 1½-inch slices
2 sweet red peppers, in ½-inch strips
1 small cauliflower, broken into flowerets
6½ cups vinegar (5% acidity)
2 cups sugar
1 fresh hot red pepper, sliced crosswise
3 Tbsps. mustard seeds
2 Tbsps. celery seeds

Dissolve salt in water; put all vegetables in large pot. Pour salt water over vegetables; cover; leave in cool place 12-18 hours; drain well. In 10-quart Dutch oven, stir together vinegar and remaining ingredients; bring to boil; cook 3 minutes. Add vegetables; reduce heat; simmer until thoroughly heated. Pack into hot sterilized jars, leaving ¼-inch headspace; cover at once with metal lids, screwing bands tight. Process in boiling water bath for 15 minutes. Very Much Worth the Effort!!

Yields 6 pints.

Charlotte Webberman, Dallas, Texas

TEXAS FACT:
The Pecan Tree, the State Tree of Texas, thrives beside Texas rivers and streams. Many of the trees are centuries old. James Stephen Hogg, Governor of Texas from 1891-95, so loved the pecan tree that he directed that one be planted by his grave, and the nuts be distributed to the people of Texas for planting throughout the state.

TEXAS BIG:
Texas has over 400 museums, and most charge no admission (those that do, charge a modest amount). The greatest concentration of world-class museums is in Fort Worth's Amon Carter Square. Museums located here include the Amon G. Carter Museum of Western Art, Kimbrell Art Museum, Fort Worth Art Center, Hall of Texas History, and the Museum of Science and History!

MEATS AND MAIN DISHES

ANN'S SENSATIONAL BEEF AND GREEN ONIONS

3 Tbsps. soy sauce
2 Tbsps. sherry
2 Tbsps. cornstarch
1 tsp. sugar

1/4 tsp. pepper
1 lb. beef, cut in strips
   (chuck or sirloin, etc.)
4 Tbsps. cooking oil

8 ozs. green onions & tops,
   sliced diagonally
1 1/2 tsps. soy sauce
2-4 drops sesame oil

To make marinade, combine first 5 ingredients; add beef for at least 20 minutes. Heat skillet or wok, add 1 tablespoon oil and onions; stir-fry for a minute. Remove onions; wipe wok/skillet with paper towel. Reheat; add rest of oil, then meat; cook 1-2 minutes; add green onions and rest of ingredients. Serve immediately. Delicious served over rice with green salad and hot, crusty bread! Just as good with salad and bread only!
Serves 4-6.

BANDIT DEVILED STEAK STRIPS

1 1/2 lbs. round steak
3 Tbsps. shortening, melted
1/2 cup flour
1/4 cup onion, chopped

1 clove garlic, minced
1 1/2 cups water
1 Tbsp. vinegar
1 tsp. prepared mustard

4 ozs. tomato sauce
1 tsp. horseradish
Salt to taste
1/4 tsp. pepper

Trim excess fat from and cut meat in 2-inch thin strips. Coat with flour. In skillet with shortening, brown meat, onion, and garlic. Stir in 1 cup water and next 6 ingredients; cover; simmer 1 hour or until meat is tender; stir occasionally. When meat is tender, stir in 1/2-cup water; scrape browned bits from bottom of pan; heat through. Serve over rice or pasta. Everyone Loves!
Serves 4-6.

"These recipes come from two of the best yet down to earth cooks that I know, Ann Rogers and Phyllis Cheesman, respectively. Both recipes are excellent, "no fail," and can be prepared quickly!!"

Jeanne Verlenden, GREAT FLAVORS OF TEXAS

BARBARA HARRIS' CHICKEN FRIED STEAK

2½ lbs. round steak, tenderized & cut into 6 equal pieces

2 cups buttermilk, in a pie plate

2 cups flour, in separate plate

Vegetable shortening, for frying

Dip each steak in buttermilk; dredge in flour; repeat process. Cook in deep fryer at 350° until golden brown, about 4-5 minutes. Serve immediately, drowned in Wonderful Cream Gravy! *Serves 6.*

WONDERFUL CREAM GRAVY

4 Tbsps. pan drippings, with "crunchy pieces" left in pan

4 Tbsps. flour

2 cups milk

Salt & pepper to taste

Add flour to drippings, and stir while browning over medium high heat. Slowly add milk; stir constantly until thickened. Add seasonings. Serve over chicken fried steak and biscuits (page 66).

"I believe that Barbara Harris, who lives in Kerrville, Texas, makes the perfect chicken fried steak! She doesn't even use salt and pepper as the buttermilk provides lots of flavor!!"

Mike Hughes, Ingram, Texas

TEXAS NOTABLE:
Fleet Admiral Chester Nimitz, the last Five Star Admiral, grew up in Fredericksburg, Texas. Nimitz was Commander-in-Chief of the Pacific War during World War II. He commanded thousands of ships, planes, and millions of men and had more military power than had been wielded by all military commanders in all previous wars!

TEXAS PLACE:
Fredericksburg is home to the Admiral Nimitz Historical State Park. The admiral requested that the park be dedicated to the two million men and women who served with him in the Pacific War. It features the lovely Garden of Peace which was given by the people of Japan. The Museum of the Pacific War, also in Fredericksburg, is the only museum of its kind in the United States.

BRANGUS MARINADE FOR BEEF BRISKET/RIBS

6 Tbsps. Morton tender quick
*   cure*
6 Tbsps. granulated sugar

1 Tbsp. dry lemon pepper
2 Tbsps. black pepper
1 Tbsp. paprika

5-6 lbs. beef brisket or ribs

Mix well first 5 ingredients; cover brisket/ribs with dry marinade; put in plastic bag; refrigerate; marinate overnight; turn at least once. Before cooking, wrap brisket in heavy foil; grill 2-3 hours over hot coals or bake in oven at 250° for 5-6 hours. Good!
Serves 8-10.

Mikey Herndon, Austin, Texas

BROWNSVILLE CHOPPED SIRLOIN OLE

2 sticks margarine
3 lbs. chopped sirloin
8 ozs. fresh green peas,
*   shelled & washed*

8 ozs. fresh green beans,
*   washed & sliced*
1 carrot, chopped
3 tomatoes, chopped

3 green onions & tops, chopped
1 lb. potatoes, chopped
1 lb. fresh mushrooms,
*   chopped*

Melt 1 stick margarine; brown meat. Separately, melt other stick margarine; saute rest of ingredients 10-12 minutes or until tender but not mushy; add to meat; cover; cook 10-12 minutes more. Serve with rice and green salad. Excellent!
Serves 6-8.

Rosita Broca, Brownsville, Texas

TEXAS PLACE AND FESTIVAL:
Brownsville is Texas' southernmost city, as well as an international seaport, airport, and railroad interchange point on Texas' border with Mexico. The city was founded in 1846 by General Zachary Taylor who established Fort Brown which is now part of Texas Southmost College.

The Charro Days Festival, held in Brownsville every February, is a vibrant early tribute to neighbors on both sides of the border and the festival's activities reflect the city's pride in its rich Mexican heritage.

BRISKET IN CHILI SAUCE AND BEER

5-7 lbs. fresh beef brisket,
excess fat removed
2 tsps. seasoned salt

1/4 tsp. seasoned pepper
2 cloves garlic, crushed
1 (12 oz.) bottle chili sauce

2 large onions, sliced
1/4 cup water
1 (12 oz.) can beer, warm

Season brisket with next 3 ingredients; place, fat side up, in roaster pan; cover with onions, chili sauce, and water. Roast, uncovered, at 300° for 1½-2 hours or until brisket is brown, basting every half hour. Pour beer over meat; cover tightly with aluminum foil; roast 3-4 hours more. When done, remove meat from gravy; refrigerate both separately. When cold, slice brisket, not quite all the way through; remove fat from gravy. Heat brisket with gravy before serving. Brisket freezes well sliced! Brisket's weight will determine length of roasting time. As briskets vary in amounts of juice released, while cooking, add small amounts of water to maintain gravy, if needed.
Serves 6-10.

Amy Levine, Fort Worth, Texas

DOTTIE'S CORN BEEF HASH

1 (12 oz.) can corn beef
1 small white onion, chopped
1 small bell pepper, chopped

3 small red potatoes, chopped
1 Tbsp. bacon grease
1/4 cup flour

Boiling water
Dash of Tabasco, optional

In skillet over medium high heat, brown first 4 ingredients in bacon grease; mix in flour. Pour in water until mixture is of desired "hash" consistency. Cover; simmer 20-25 minutes over low heat or until potatoes are tender. Wonderful served over buttered bread with a salad.
Serves 4.

Joy E. Levens, San Antonio, Texas

TEXAS FACT:
The cattle industry of the United States began in Texas with long-horned cattle. Texas cattlemen drove their herds to Missouri and Kansas for shipment by railroad. The most widely used cattle trails were the Chisholm and Western Trails. The Chisholm Trail began at the Mexican Border and ended in Abilene, Kansas. The Western Trail connected West Texas and Dodge City, Kansas.

CATTLE COUNTRY HAMBURGER LASAGNA

12 ozs. lasagna noodles,
  cooked per pkg.'s
  directions & drained
2 lbs. ground round
2 cloves garlic, crushed
2 tsps. sugar

Salt & pepper to taste
4 (8 oz.) cans tomato sauce
1 (8 oz.) pkg. cream cheese
8 green onions & tops,
  chopped
1 (8 oz.) carton sour cream

8 ozs. cottage cheese
2 tsps. Italian seasoning
3 fresh tomatoes, sliced
2 cups Cheddar cheese, grated

In skillet, brown meat and garlic; drain; add sugar and seasonings; cook until well blended, 2-4 minutes; add tomato sauce; simmer, covered, 15 minutes. Separately, mix well next 5 ingredients. In greased 4-quart oblong casserole, layer as follows: half noodles, half meat, half cheese mixture. Repeat layering once. Arrange tomatoes on top; cover with grated cheese. Bake at 350°, uncovered, for 40 minutes; remove; let stand 10 minutes; cut into squares. Superb!
Serves 10-12. (Easily halved)

EL PASO TORTILLA LASAGNA

1 lb. lean ground beef
1 large onion, chopped
1 (10½ oz.) can cream of
  chicken soup
4 Tbsps. chili powder

1 (8 oz.) can tomato sauce
1 (4 oz.) can chopped green
  chilies
1 (10 oz.) can tomatoes, chopped
1 tsp. cumin

1 tsp. salt
½ tsp. pepper
12 flour tortillas (page 78)
1 lb. Monterey Jack cheese,
  grated

In pan, brown meat and onions; drain. Add next 8 ingredients; stir well; cook until blended, about 10 minutes. In greased 9x13-inch baking dish, place 6 tortillas and half the sauce; top with half the cheese. Repeat layering once. Bake at 350° for 30-40 minutes. Casserole may be refrigerated or frozen before baking. If frozen, let thaw before baking. A Wonderful Busy Day Dish!!
Serves 8.

Diane Sullivan, El Paso, Texas

TEXAS TREASURE:
El Paso is the home of the Border Patrol Museum which is the only museum in the United States that presents the rich heritage of the U.S. Border Patrol.

COUSIN LACEY'S PRIME RIB ROAST

1 rib roast   *Seasoned salt*   *Seasoned pepper*

Cooking time is determined by roast's weight; have roast cut to desired size. Preheat oven to 500°. Place roast in pan ribs side down; sprinkle with salt and pepper. Cook roast 5 minutes per pound; when cooked per pound time, turn off oven; leave roast in oven for 1-2 hours (no less than 1, no longer than 2!). Don't open oven doors from time roast is put in oven until serving time! When ready to serve, remove and slice. Roast will be rare and juicy! For medium rare, add 5 minutes to total cooking time; for medium, add 10 minutes to total cooking time at 500°.

MARTHA LOU'S VEAL CHOPS IN WINE

4 Tbsps. butter	*¾ cup red wine*	*3 Tbsps. butter*
¼ cup flour	*1 (10½ oz.) can condensed*	*4 veal loin chops, 1¼-inch thick,*
½ tsp. salt	*beef bouillon*	*excess fat trimmed, & each*
Pinch of pepper	*½ lb. fresh mushrooms, sliced*	*wiped with damp paper towel*
½ tsp. rosemary	*2 Tbsps. lemon juice*	*1½ cups onion, sliced*
1 tsp. fresh chives, snipped	*1 Tbsp. butter*	*1 clove garlic, minced*

In saucepan, melt butter; remove from heat; stir in next 5 ingredients. Add enough wine to bouillon to make 2 cups. Gradually, stir wine mixture into flour mixture; stir occasionally; bring to boil; remove from heat. Separately, toss mushrooms with lemon juice; saute in 1 tablespoon butter about 5 minutes; set aside. In skillet, heat 3 tablespoons butter; brown chops on both sides. Move chops to side of skillet; add onion and garlic; saute until golden; add ½-cup wine mixture and mushrooms; simmer, covered, over low heat, for 30 minutes or until chops are tender; add more wine mixture as needed. Place chops on platter; stir any remaining wine mixture into skillet; mix well; reheat; pour over chops. Sumptuously Elegant!

Serves 4 divinely!

Martha Lou Rugeley, Wichita Falls, Texas

TEXAS BIG:
Texas is the leading producer of beef in the United States and has more than 180,000 farms and ranches which cover about 82% of the state's land area!

BROKEN ARROW RANCH CHILI

3 lbs. lean chuck, coarsely ground
2 Tbsps. vegetable oil
1 (12 oz.) can beer
1 large onion, chopped
3 garlic cloves, finely chopped
1 jalapeno pepper, finely chopped
4 tsps. cumin
1 Tbsp. paprika
5 Tbsps. chili powder
1 tsp. salt
1/4 tsp. black pepper

In heavy pot (with tight fitting lid), brown beef in oil. Add half can beer; cook, covered, over low heat for an hour; stir occasionally to prevent sticking. Drain; put drippings into skillet; saute onion, garlic, and jalapeno in drippings. Pour sauteed vegetables with drippings over beef; add rest of ingredients; stir to blend. Cover; cook over low heat for 1-1½ hours, adding rest of beer as needed. Super and Definitely Texas!
Serves 8-10. (Easily doubled/halved)

Mike Hughes, Ingram, Texas

LONE STAR CHILI

1 Tbsp. corn oil
3 garlic cloves, crushed
1 large onion, chopped
2 lbs. ground beef, chili ground
1 Tbsp. ground cumin
4 Tbsps. chili powder
1 tsp. salt
1/4 tsp. black pepper
2 Tbsps. flour
3 cups water, boiling

In skillet, heat oil; soften, but don't brown, garlic and onion. Add beef; cook slowly for 15 minutes (beef will begin to brown); drain. Add next 5 ingredients; stir well for 2-3 minutes; add water. Continue to cook over low heat for 45-50 minutes more. Serve with Minnie's Corn Fritters (page 85). Super Busy Day Dish!!
Serves 6-8. (Easily doubled/halved)

Linda Wingartern, Fort Worth, Texas

TEXAS FACT:
The Cowtown Coliseum in Fort Worth was the site of the very first indoor rodeo in 1917!

EASY POT ROAST A LA CHILI BEANS

3-4 lbs. beef chuck roast
Salt & pepper to taste
1-2 Tbsps. vegetable oil
2 Tbsps. brown sugar

2 Tbsps. dry mustard
1½ tsps. paprika
¼-½ tsp. chili powder
1 medium onion, chopped

1 (15½ oz.) can chili-style
beans
1 Tbsp. flour

Season roast with salt and pepper. In Dutch oven, brown meat on all sides in hot oil. Combine next 4 ingredients; rub over surface of meat; top with beans and onion. Cover; bake at 350° for 2-2½ hours or until tender. Remove roast to warm platter; skim off fat. Add enough water to pan drippings to make 1 cup liquid. Combine flour with 2 tablespoons water; add to pan juice. Cook until bubbly to make gravy; pour over roast. Easy and Delicious!!
Serves 6-8.

Charlotte Webberman, Dallas, Texas

MANNY'S PICADILLO
(Manny's Chopped Meat)

4-5 Tbsps. olive oil
1 large onion, chopped
½ bell pepper, chopped
3 cloves garlic, crushed

2 lbs. lean ground chuck
Salt & pepper to taste
2 bay leaves
2 (8 oz.) cans tomato sauce

1 cup fresh mushrooms, sliced
1 (10 oz.) pkg. frozen green
peas, cooked
1 cup uncooked rice, cooked

In oil in skillet, saute next 3 ingredients. Separately, brown beef with salt and pepper; drain. Add meat to sauteed mixture; stir; add bay leaves and next 2 ingredients; cover; simmer 30 minutes. If desired, add a little water. Serve over rice, and top with peas.
Serves 6. (Easily doubled/halved)

"This recipe has been in my family for years. My brother-in-law, Manny, introduced this version of the Spanish-style recipe. It's an easy, good way to dress up ground beef!"

Irma Furnish, New Braunfels, Texas

FAJITA AND RIB PACHANGA FOR FIFTY

20 lbs. fajitas, skirt or flank
    steak, skin & fat removed
25 finger ribs, cut in half
Salt & pepper to taste

Garlic powder to taste
3 qts. barbeque sauce
    (3 qts. = 12 cups)
20 lbs. onion, sliced

15 bell peppers, cut in thin,
    long strips
Warmer & charcoal

Season beef and ribs with next 2 ingredients; put over hot coals; cook to medium or medium well. When done, slice lengthwise into strips; put in warmer heated to 120°; put onions and peppers under and over meat; cover with 6 cups barbecue sauce; leave in warmer 1-2 hours. Serve with rest of sauce, beans (page 81), and slaw (page 84). Delightful!
Serves 50 or thereabouts!

George A. Moreno and Judge Filemon B. Vela, Brownsville, Texas

FORT WORTH HICKORY BARBECUE SAUCE

1/4 cup onion, finely minced
1 Tbsp. brown sugar
1 Tbsp. mustard seed
2 tsps. paprika
1 clove garlic, pressed
1 tsp. pepper

1/2 tsp. salt
1/4 tsp. ground cloves
1 bay leaf
2 Tbsps. Worcestershire sauce
1 cup catsup
1/2 cup water

1/4 cup olive oil
1/3 cup tarragon vinegar
1 tsp. oregano
1 tsp. chili powder
2-3 drops liquid smoke,
    optional

In saucepan, combine well all ingredients. Simmer for about 25 minutes; stir occasionally; remove bay leaf. Wonderful Over Beef or Pork!!
Yields 2 cups.

Linda Wingartern, Fort Worth, Texas

TEXAS FACT:
The flags of six countries have flown over the land we call Texas! They are: Spain (1519-1685; 1690-1821); France (1685-1690); Mexico (1821-1836); The Texas Republic (1836-1845); The Confederate States of America (1861-1865); The United States of America (1845-1861; 1865-The Present).

MAGNIFICENT BROILED STEAK TEXICAN

1 large sirloin, rib eye *or* porterhouse steak, 1½-inch thick (enough to serve 4-6)	2-3 tsps. fresh ginger, minced	1¼ tsps. dry mustard
	1 tsp. black pepper	3 tsps. Worcestershire sauce
	Seasoned salt to taste	½ tsp. paprika
¼-½ cup olive oil	Garlic powder to taste	
	5 Tbsps. butter, softened	

Rub oil generously into both sides of steak. Loosely wrap in plastic wrap; let stand at room temperature for 2-3 hours. Before broiling, sprinkle 1 side with ½ of ginger. Broil, ginger side to heat, for 5-6 minutes; sprinkle broiled side with next 3 seasonings; turn; sprinkle uncooked side with ½ of ginger and seasonings; broil 3-4 minutes. Make paste of rest of ingredients; remove meat to hot serving platter; spread paste over each side of steak. Enjoy the Best!!

MAMA GRANDES ENCHILADAS SAUCE

2 lbs. lean ground chuck	1 oz. garlic powder	2 cups all purpose flour
16 ozs. salad oil	4 ozs. chili powder	1 gallon hot water
1-3 ozs. salt	1 oz. ground cumin	

In large pot, saute meat in oil until brown. Add rest of ingredients in the order listed; stir. Over medium heat, cook sauce for about 25 minutes or until see red bubbles coming out of sauce; stir often. When bubbles appear, continue to cook and stir for 5 minutes more. That's All There Is To It! Outstanding!

Makes enough for a small army!

"This recipe is over 100 years old. It was my grandmother's recipe, and I have used it for more than 30 years and, in my business, served thousands of enchiladas! My grandmother was quite simply the best cook I've ever known! The sauce is excellent for Frito pies, macaroni and cheese, taco salad, cheese omelets, chicken casseroles, bean dips, and tamale pies! It is not a hot-hot/spicy sauce but rather one that can be enjoyed by just about everyone!"

Richard S. Vasquez, R.J.'s RESTAURANT, Uvalde, Texas

TEXAS FAJITA FEAST

3 lbs. skirt steak _or_ 8 chicken
  breasts, boned & skinned
1½ cups picante sauce (page
  99*)
1½ cups bottled Italian
  dressing
3 Tbsps. lemon juice

1½ tsps. garlic powder
4 Tbsps. green onions & tops,
  chopped
1½ tsps. black pepper
1½ tsps. celery salt
8-10 flour tortillas (page 78*)
Salsa (page 101*)

Guacamole (page 6,*
  omit tomatoes)
2 onions, sliced & grilled
3-4 tomatoes, chopped
1 lb. Cheddar cheese, grated
1 (8 oz.) carton sour cream

Remove any fat from meat; wipe dry with paper towels; put meat in shallow dish. Make
marinade by combining picante sauce and next 6 ingredients; pour over meat; refrigerate;
marinate overnight or at least 6 hours. Grill meat over hot coals until chicken is done or meat
is cooked sufficiently (per your taste); cut meat diagonally into thin strips; fold several slices
into a warm flour tortilla with salsa, guacamole, onions, tomatoes, cheese, and sour cream in
any desired combinations and amounts! Enjoy!
Serves 8 heartily!!

Barbara Jones, Bonham, Texas

**We have included page numbers of recipes for these ingredients for your Fajita Feast! If you
have a little spare time, go for broke, and make everything from scratch! If you have no time,
your local supermarket will have some pretty good substitutes! Have fun and success! Flank
steak also makes fine fajitas! The Editors*

TEXAS NOTABLE:
*Sam Rayburn called Texas and more particularly Bonham, Texas, home throughout his long and
distinguished career in public service. "Mister Sam" served as Speaker of the House of Representatives
longer than anyone else in American history. His home, in Bonham, has been restored and is open to
the public as is the Sam Rayburn Library which features an exact replica of Speaker Rayburn's office
in Washington D.C.*

LAMB ON THE GRILL

5 lb. leg of lamb, boned &
    butterflied (Butcher will
    do. Do **not** have lamb tied.)

Juice of 1 lemon
1/4 cup soy sauce
2 cloves garlic, minced

1/4 cup fresh rosemary on the
    stem _or_ 1 tsp. dried
Salt & pepper to taste

Combine lemon and rest of ingredients; rub into lamb. Let lamb stand for 1-3 hours. Grill over hot charcoal until inside is pink, about 2½-3 hours (will register 180° on meat thermometer). Excellent with green salad (page 45) or fresh fruit salad (page 46)!
Serves 6-8.

Linda Waterman, Dallas, Texas

HIGH PLAINS HAM LOAF

3 lbs. ham, finely ground
2 lbs. pork, finely ground
1 tsp. pepper
1 tsp. paprika
3 eggs

1 (10¾ oz.) can tomato soup
2/3 cup cracker crumbs
1/3 cup whipping cream,
    whipped

1/3 cup mayonnaise
1/3 cup mustard

To make loaf, mix well first 7 ingredients. Place in greased loaf pan; bake at 300° for 1½ hours. Make sauce by folding mayonnaise and mustard into cream. To serve, slice loaf; spoon sauce over slices. Outstanding!
Serves 10-12.

Marguerite Griner Melson, Abilene, Texas

TEXAS PLACE:
The Dallas Zoo is well known as one of the ten best zoos in the United States and has more than 2,000 bird and animal species. The Reptile House includes one of the world's largest collections of rattlesnakes!

TEXAS BIG:
The highest price ever paid for a hog was, of course, in Texas! On March 5, 1985, E.A. "Bud" Olson of Phil Bonzio, Texas, paid $56,000 to Jeffrey Roemisch of Hermleigh, Texas, for a cross-bred barrow hog named "Bud!!"

CISCO GRILL'S BLACK BEAN CHILI

4 cups dried black beans,
 sorted & rinsed
½ lb. bulk pork sausage,
 crumbled
2 large onions, finely chopped
2 cloves garlic, minced
2 Tbsps. cumin

2 Tbsps. oregano
1½ cups bell pepper, finely
 chopped
1 tsp. cayenne pepper
1½ Tbsps. paprika
1 tsp. salt
4 ozs. canned jalapenos

⅔ cup sour cream
½ cup green onions, finely
 chopped
½ lb. Monterey Jack cheese,
 grated
8 sprigs cilantro for garnish

In pot, cover beans with water until beans are 3-4 inches under water; cover; bring to boil. Reduce heat; simmer for 2 hours or until beans are tender. Add water if bean tops begin to show. When done, drain: reserve cup of bean liquid; add back to beans. In skillet, cook sausage; add next 9 ingredients. Cook for 10 minutes; add to beans; heat through. To serve, place 1 ounce cheese in bowl; add 1 cup chili; top with sour cream; sprinkle with green onions; top with cilantro. *Serves 8.*

Susan and Marc Hall, CISCO GRILL RESTAURANT, Dallas, Texas

MARVELOUS PORK TENDERS WITH ORANGE GLAZE

2½ lbs. pork tenderloin
¼ cup Worcestershire sauce
2 tsps. dry mustard

¾ cup brown sugar, firmly
 packed
2 Tbsps. vinegar

2 Tbsps. cornstarch
¾ cup orange juice
Salt & pepper to taste

In refrigerator, marinate overnight pork in Worcestershire in sealed plastic bag. To make glaze, mix well next 5 ingredients; cook over medium heat; stir often until mixture thickens; set aside. Season pork; place on grill over hot charcoal; grill 10 minutes; turn; brush cooked side with glaze; grill 10 minutes; remove. Place tenders in baking dish; cover with rest of glaze; hold in 250° oven until serving time (can be up to 1½ hours). Before serving, slice into ½-inch thick slices. Serve with glaze, Artichoke Rice Salad (page 40) and hot, crusty bread. A Marvelous Summer Supper Dish! *Serves 6-8.*

John Crank, Dallas, Texas

SOUTHWESTERN GRILLED PORK

1/4 cup fresh lime juice
1 Tbsp. lemon juice
1 1/2 tsps. lime peel, grated
2 tsps. fresh ginger, peeled
& minced

1 Tbsp. sugar
3 Tbsps. fresh cilantro,
minced
1/3 cup olive oil
3 cloves garlic, minced

2 lbs. boneless pork loin,
trimmed & butterflied
Salt & pepper to taste

Mix first 8 ingredients to make marinade; pour over pork; marinate several hours or in refrigerator overnight. Season to taste; grill over hot coals, about 15 minutes per-inch-thickness per side. Slice; serve with Southwestern Sauce (below).
Serves 6.

SOUTHWESTERN SAUCE

1/3 cup unsalted butter, melted
1 Tbsp. fresh lime juice

1/2 tsp. lime peel, grated
1 Tbsp. parsley, minced

2 Tbsps. cilantro, minced
Salt to taste

In saucepan, combine all ingredients; heat. Serve with grilled pork. This sauce is also delicious with baked and roasted pork! A Truly Texas Taste!!

Ginger Carlin, Dallas, Texas

TEXAS TREASURE:
Located in the Panhandle, Muleshoe, Texas, is the site of the National Monument to Mules! The strength and dependability of mules helped in the settlement of Texas and the American West. Donations for this memorial came from individuals throughout the United States and the world, including a donation of 21 cents from a mule driver in Uzbekistan (formerly part of the Soviet Union)!!

TEXAS FESTIVALS:
The International Bar-B-Q Cookoff, held in Taylor, Texas, each year in August, features trophies in the pork, sausage, beef, poultry, wild game, mutton, goat, seafood, and sauce categories!

The West Texas Fair, held annually in Abilene for 10 days in mid-September, features exhibits and amusements reflecting Abilene's early days as well as the modern attractions of West Texas!

ADOLPHUS HOTEL ROASTED QUAIL

1/8 cup olive oil	Salt & pepper to taste	1 egg yolk
1 tsp. garlic	1 lb. white chicken meat	4 quail
6 fresh <u>or</u> canned artichoke hearts, finely chopped	3/4 cup heavy cream	4 grape leaves
1 tsp. shallots	1/4 cup reduced chicken glaze, chilled	

In skillet, heat oil; saute next 3 ingredients and seasonings for 5 minutes; remove; chill. In food processor with metal blade, combine chicken, and next 3 ingredients; blend until completely smooth. Fold in artichoke mixture; cool stuffing mixture. Place stuffing in pastry bag fitted with plain round tip; pipe into quail's cavity; chill immediately. About 1-2 hours before serving, quail should be seared on all sides in pan over medium heat until golden brown; then, wrapped in grape leaves; chill until ready to roast. Roast quail at 375° for 15 minutes or until done. (Grape leaves come in a jar and are available in specialty stores and some supermarkets.)
Serves 4 elegantly!

Kevin Garvin, Executive Chef, The French Room, ADOLPHUS HOTEL, Dallas, Texas

TEXAS PLACE:
The Adolphus Hotel has been a Dallas landmark for almost 80 years! The hotel is a unique creation of fortune and flamboyance from an extravagant age. The original hotel was built by beer baron, Adolphus Bush, who spared no expense in erecting in Dallas what critics have called "the most beautiful building west of Venice!"

TEXAS TREASURE:
Nacogdoches, located in East Texas, is a city of "firsts." It was the first settlement in Texas, established in 1778! It has the oldest public thoroughfare in the United States which is today called North Street! Texas' first newspaper, Gaceta de Tejas, began publication in Nacogdoches. The city is also home to Millards Crossing which is a group of restored 19th century buildings furnished with antiques and pioneer memorabilia!

BUSY DAY CHICKEN DIVAN

4 chicken breasts, skinned, cooked, boned, & chopped
1 (10 oz.) pkg. frozen broccoli, cooked per pkg.'s directions
1 (10¾ oz.) can cream of chicken soup
½ cup mayonnaise
2 Tbsps. lemon juice
½ tsp. curry powder
1 cup Cheddar cheese, grated
¾ cup bread crumbs
1 Tbsp. butter

In a 1½-quart casserole, spread broccoli; top with chicken. Separately, mix soup with next 3 ingredients; pour over chicken; sprinkle cheese over soup; top with crumbs; dot with butter. Bake at 350°, covered, for 30 minutes. Great Meal in One Dish!
Serves 4.

Dianne Riatigue, San Antonio, Texas

CACTUS COUNTRY CHICKEN CILANTRO

1 small onion, chopped
1 clove garlic, crushed
2 Tbsps. butter
2 Tbsps. salad oil
4 whole chicken breasts, split, boned & cut in 1-inch pieces
1 tsp. salt
¼ tsp. pepper
2 Tbsps. cilantro, chopped
2 cups rice, cooked
Lemon wedges

In skillet, cook onion and garlic in butter and oil until tender; add chicken, salt and pepper; cook, and stir over medium high heat until done, about 5 minutes; stir in cilantro; pour pan juices over chicken. Serve with/over rice, garnished with lemon wedges. Good and Easy!
Serves 4.

Mary Denny, San Antonio, Texas

TEXAS PLACE:
Located in deep Southwest Texas, the heart of Cactus Country, Langtry, Texas, is called home by a population of 30! Langtry is rich in Texas history for Langtry was home to Judge Roy Bean, who during the 1880's was known as the only "Law West of the Pecos." The State of Texas maintains the Judge Roy Bean Visitor Center there which preserves the historic site where Judge Bean ruled with a high-handed, but appropriate brand of homespun law! The center also features a marvelous cactus garden which displays the flora of the Southwest.

CAMILLE'S CHICKEN PICCATA

3 Tbsps. flour
1/2 tsp. salt plus 1/4 tsp. pepper
6 chicken breasts, skinned & boned

6 Tbsps. margarine
1/3 cup dry white wine
4 Tbsps. lemon juice

1 Tbsp. parsley, chopped
6 lemon slices

In pie plate, combine first 2 ingredients; coat chicken with flour mixture. In skillet over medium high heat, melt 4 tablespoons margarine. Brown chicken for 4 minutes each side or until chicken is cooked through; remove to warm platter. In same skillet, melt remaining margarine; add wine and juice; cook 2-3 minutes; scrape up any browned particles. Add parsley; spoon over chicken. Serve with lemon slices. Good!

Serves 6.

Camille Warmington, Houston, Texas

CAROLANN'S CHICKEN FLAUTAS

2 (each) chicken breasts, legs, & thighs, cooked, boned, & meat shredded
1/2 medium green pepper, chopped
1 Tbsp. scallions, chopped
1 small tomato, chopped

2 tsps. cilantro, chopped
Salt & pepper to taste
1/8 tsp. ground cumin
2 Tbsps. tomato paste
1/2 cup chicken broth
Oil for frying
24 corn tortillas (page 78)

TOPPING:
1 medium avocado, mashed, with pinch salt & lemon juice
1 small tomato, chopped
1 (8 oz.) carton sour cream

Mix chicken with next 8 ingredients. In skillet, heat tortillas in oil just long enough to soften for rolling. Take 1 tortilla at a time, put 1 tablespoon chicken mixture across 1 end of tortilla, roll tortilla very tightly until about the size of a finger, turn seam side down, wrap with plastic wrap, and place seam side down in baking dish. Repeat this process with each tortilla. Put wrapped tortillas in dish in freezer. Let freeze. To cook, remove plastic wrap; place 2-3 frozen tortillas into deep hot oil; fry about 2 minutes or until brown and crisp. Remove, keep warm in 200° oven until all are cooked. Serve immediately; top each with avocado, dollop of sour cream and tomato. Nothing better!

Makes 24 flautas.

Carolann Gerescher, San Antonio, Texas

CHICKEN BREASTS MARSALA WITH FETTUCINE

4 ozs. dried porcini
  mushrooms or mushrooms
4 Tbsps. butter, melted
4 chicken breasts, skinned &
  boned

1 clove garlic, minced
½ cup dry Marsala wine
1 lb. Italian cream cheese or
  cream cheese
2 Tbsps. parsley, minced

¼ lb. Montasio (sharp goat
  cheese), grated
1 lb. fresh fettucine, cooked,
  drained, & hot
Fresh parsley for garnish

Soften mushrooms in hot water; rinse 2-3 times to clean; strain, reserving first "water strained." In skillet, saute chicken (4-5 minutes each side) and garlic in butter; remove. To same skillet, add wine and reserved "mushroom water." Bring to boil; scrape up browned particles. Reduce heat to medium; simmer 1-2 minutes. Add cream cheese to wine mixture; melt; add mushrooms and parsley. Toss pasta with wine sauce; sprinkle with goat cheese; toss. Serve chicken over fettucine garnished with parsley. Excellent!
Serves 4 divinely!

CHICKEN BREASTS MOZZARELLA

4 chicken breasts, skinned
  & boned
2 Tbsps. butter
¼ cup white wine

1 tsp. fresh tarragon, chopped
  or ¼ tsp. dried
½ lb. Mozzarella, sliced
Salt & pepper to taste

Fresh tarragon sprigs for
  garnish

In skillet over medium heat, saute breasts in butter until golden brown all over. Add wine; let simmer a minute. Top breasts with cheese and tarragon. Cover pan; remove from heat; let stand 3-5 minutes. Season, garnish, and enjoy!!
Serves 4 wonderfully!

Paula Lambert, Dallas, Texas

Paula's Mozzarella Company provides fresh cheeses to top restaurants throughout the United States! The cheeses are available to the rest of us by mail order.

CHICKEN MARENGO

1/4 cup flour
1/2 tsp. salt
1/4 tsp. pepper
1/2 tsp. tarragon
1 fryer, cut into pieces

2 Tbsps. butter
1 Tbsp. cooking oil
1/4 cup dry white wine
1/4 cup chicken broth
8 ozs. canned tomatoes

1 clove garlic
4 mushrooms, sliced
2 Tbsps. fresh parsley,
    chopped for garnish

In bag, shake together well first 4 ingredients. Dredge chicken in flour mixture until well coated. In skillet, heat butter and oil; saute chicken pieces until brown on all sides. Transfer to 1½-quart casserole. In same skillet, mix drippings with mixture from bag; slowly, stir in wine and broth; cook, stirring until sauce is smooth and thickened. Pour over chicken; add next 3 ingredients; cover; cook at 350° for 50-55 minutes. Garnish with parsley. Serve over rice or pasta. Excellent!

Serves 4.   Jane Findling, San Antonio, Texas

CHICKEN MEXICAN SUPREME

8-10 whole chicken breasts
2 Tbsps. butter
1 onion, chopped
2 bell peppers, chopped
1 clove garlic, minced

1 (1 lb.) can tomatoes
1 tsp. chili powder
1/2 tsp. black pepper
8 ozs. fresh mushrooms, sliced
4 Tbsps. fresh parsley, chopped

1 tsp. sugar
1/2 tsp. oregano
2 Tbsps. flour, dissolved in
    1 Tbsp. water

Simmer chicken in salted water until tender; let cool; bone; reserve broth. In skillet with butter, saute next 3 ingredients; add to 2 cups broth. To broth mixture, add tomatoes and next 6 ingredients; cook over medium heat 15 minutes; thicken with flour mixture. Put chicken in shallow baking dish; cover with sauce; bake at 400° for 30 minutes. Delicious!

Serves 6-8.

"This dish was served at the White House while Lyndon Johnson was President! It was one of the President's favorite recipes!! It's a favorite in our family too!"

Shirley Bishop, Houston, Texas

DELICIOUS CHICKEN WITH MUSHROOM SAUCE

10 chicken breasts, boneless & skinned	1 onion, chopped	2 Tbsps. flour
3 cups Italian bread crumbs	1 lb. fresh mushrooms, sliced	2 Tbsps. Dijon mustard
1/2 cup olive oil	1/4 cup butter	2 cups whipping cream
1 garlic clove	1/2 cup parsley, chopped	2 Tbsps. lemon juice
	5 green onions, chopped	

Roll chicken in bread crumbs. In skillet, heat oil and garlic to medium hot; cook chicken on both sides until golden brown; set aside. Saute onions and mushrooms in butter; add next 4 ingredients; gradually, stir in cream. Cook until thick, but do not boil! Add lemon juice; pour sauce over warm chicken. Serve at once.

Serves 10.   **Charlotte Brunette, Wichita Falls, Texas**

DELICIOUS DIJON CHICKEN

2 Tbsps. butter, melted	1/2 cup dry white wine	1/2 tsp. salt
2 cloves garlic	1/4 cup water	1/4 tsp. pepper
4 chicken breasts, skinned & boned	2 Tbsps. Dijon mustard	1/4 cup fresh parsley, chopped
	1/2 tsp. dill	

In skillet over medium heat, saute garlic in butter 2 minutes or until soft; brown chicken 3 minutes on each side. Transfer to 1½-quart shallow baking dish. To skillet, add next 6 ingredients; bring to boil; cook a minute. Pour over chicken; cover; bake at 325° for 30 minutes. Add parsley; baste chicken with sauce; cook 5 minutes more.

Serves 4.   **Susan Bagwell, Dallas, Texas**

Both the above chicken dishes have two things in common. Both are delicious and both use Dijon mustard. They were both good enough and different enough that each had to be included in GREAT FLAVORS OF TEXAS!!

TEXAS FACT:
In 1964, the Manned Space Craft Center in Houston became the permanent headquarters for the United States' astronauts. In 1973, the center was renamed the Lyndon Baines Johnson Space Center after President Lyndon Johnson, a Texas native, who served as the 36th President of the United States.

127

DALLAS' SPIRITED CHICKEN

6 chicken breasts, skinned, boned, & sprinkled with ⅓ cup bourbon
4 Tbsps. butter, melted
1 carrot, cut in 2-inch long thin strips
2 ozs. Proscuitto, sliced in long, thin strips, optional
1 leek, rinsed, white/green parts cut in 2-inch long narrow strips
Salt & white pepper to taste
2 Tbsps. butter
1 Tbsp. bourbon
1 tsp. lemon juice

Refrigerate "sprinkled chicken" 20 minutes or more. Then, in skillet over medium high heat, saute breasts in butter 3-4 minutes on each side; remove; put chicken in pan; keep warm. In same skillet, saute for a minute next two ingredients; toss to cook uniformly; add leek strips; cook a minute. Spoon a mound of vegetables over each breast. Add rest of ingredients to drippings in skillet; whisk well. Drizzle over vegetables and chicken. Good!
Serves 6.

Claudia Erdmann, Dallas, Texas

GRANITE MOUNTAIN CHICKEN SPAGHETTI

1 stick butter
½ cup flour
1 tsp. salt
1 cup cream
3 cups milk
1 cup chicken broth
1 lb. Velveeta, cut in pieces
2-3 cups chicken, cooked, boned, & chopped
½ cup mushrooms, sauteed in 1 Tbsp. butter
1 (8½ oz.) can water chestnuts, drained
¼ cup pimento, cut in strips
½ cup almonds
¼ cup sherry
12 ozs. spaghetti, cooked per pkg.'s directions

In top of double boiler, melt butter; add flour and salt; cook; stir often, until smooth and bubbly; add next 3 ingredients; stir until thickened; cook 30 minutes; stir occasionally. Add cheese; stir until melted. Separately, combine next 6 ingredients; stir in spaghetti; add hot cheese sauce; gently stir.
Serves 8-10.

Donna Spaar, Marble Falls, Texas

TEXAS FACT:
The source of Texas' famed pink granite is in Marble Falls! Granite Mountain, just north of Marble Falls, is a huge dome of high quality pink and red granite. Quarrying of the mountain began in the 1880's for the construction of Texas' Capitol Building.

GREEN CHICKEN ENCHILADAS

1 lb. bag spinach, cleaned well	1 Tbsp. flour	1 cup ripe olives, chopped
1 (14½ oz.) can chicken broth	1 large onion, halved &	4 cups chicken, cooked
1 clove garlic, crushed	chopped	1 (20 count) pkg. flour
2 (10¾ oz.) cans cream of	1½ cups fresh mushrooms,	tortillas
mushroom soup	sliced	8 ozs. Cheddar cheese, grated
2 (4 oz.) cans green chilies	2 lbs. cottage cheese	2 (8 oz.) cartons sour cream

In blender, mix, until chopped, spinach and broth. In saucepan, combine spinach mixture with next 4 ingredients, ½ of onion, and ½ cup mushrooms; bring to boil; stir constantly; remove from heat. Separately, combine cottage cheese, ½ onions, rest of mushrooms, and olives; add 1 cup spinach mixture; mix. Chop chicken; add to mixture. Grease 3 7x11-inch pyrex dishes; spread tortillas (6-7 per dish) in dishes. Fill each tortilla with 2 tablespoons cottage cheese filling; roll tortillas up; cover with remaining spinach sauce. Cook at 350° for about 20 minutes or until bubbly; spread cheese on top; return to oven until cheese melts; top with sour cream; return to oven 5 minutes more. The Absolute Best One Dish Meal!!

Serves 10-12 generously!

HOUSTON BARBECUED CHICKEN

½ cup Wesson oil	⅓ cup lemon juice	Garlic salt to taste
¾ cup onion, chopped	4 Tbsps. Worcestershire sauce	2 broiler chickens, split in
1 cup tomato catsup	3 Tbsps. sugar	half & cleaned
½ cup water	2 Tbsps. prepared mustard	
¼ tsp. chili powder	Salt & pepper to taste	

In skillet, saute onions in oil until soft. Add next 9 ingredients; simmer, covered 15 minutes. Brush chicken with sauce; place over hot coals or under broiler; baste chicken every 5 minutes or so; after 15 minutes, turn; baste; baste every 5 minutes for 15 minutes more; turn; repeat process once more. Heat remaining sauce; pour over chicken. Super!

Serves 4.

C.Y. Wilson, Houston, Texas

KING RANCH CASSEROLE

1 large fryer, cooked & boned
1 (10¾ oz.) can cream of
*   chicken soup*
1 (14½ oz.) can chicken broth

1 (10¾ oz.) can cream of
*   mushroom soup*
4 ozs. Ro-tel tomatoes & hot
*   peppers*

1½ cups cheese, grated
1 (12 oz.) pkg. Fritos, crushed
1 onion, chopped
½ cup cheese, grated

In bowl, mix well first five ingredients. In greased 2½-3-quart casserole, layer as follows: ½ chicken mixture, ½ Fritos, ½ cheese, ½ onion. Repeat layering once; put rest of cheese on top; bake at 350° for 20 minutes or until lightly browned. Easy And Delicious!
Serves 8.

Mary J. Harty, Lubbock, Texas

LEMON CHICKEN DIVINE

5 chicken breasts, cooked &
*   cooled in the broth; boned*
*   & skinned*
10 dried black mushrooms, if
*   available, or mushrooms*
2 Tbsps. vegetable oil

⅓ cup fresh ginger, cut in
*   long thin strips*
¼ cup red or green chili
*   peppers, cut in thin strips*
¼ cup lemon peel, cut in strips
2 Tbsps. sugar

½ cup fresh lemon juice
Pinch of salt
1 Tbsp. lemon peel, finely
*   grated*
2 tsps. lemon extract

Soak mushrooms in very hot water for 30 minutes. Cut chicken meat in 1-inch cubes. Strain broth into 1 cup measure; use mushroom liquid, if necessary, to make 1 cup. Squeeze mushrooms dry; remove stems; slice caps into thin shreds. In skillet or wok, heat oil over medium heat; add mushrooms and ginger; stir fry a minute. Add next 3 ingredients; stir; add broth; bring to boil; mix in well juice; season; add chicken; stir for 30 seconds. Remove chicken only to serving dish; blend peel and extract into sauce; pour over chicken. Serve at room temperature or chilled. Either Way, Heavenly!
Serves 5.

Amy Levine, Austin, Texas

TEXAS BIG:
The largest ranch in the continental United States is the King Ranch which covers all or part of four Texas counties with over 823,000 acres!

LONGHORN CHICKEN CASSEROLE

4 cups chicken, cooked, boned, & chopped
4 cups celery, chopped
1 cup almonds, toasted & chopped
2 tsps. salt
3/4 tsp. cracked pepper
1/2 cup onion, grated
1/3 cup lemon juice
1 tsp. Accent, optional
1 3/4 cups mayonnaise
4 tsps. Tabasco
1 cup Cheddar cheese, grated
1 cup potato chips, crushed
Parmesan cheese
Paprika

Mix well first 10 ingredients. Pour into 3-quart greased casserole; sprinkle with cheese; top with potato chips to 1/4-inch thick; sprinkle with Parmesan; sprinkle paprika over all. Bake at 350° for 35-40 minutes or until cooked through with bubbly top. Good!
Serves 10.
Marti Turner, Houston, Texas

MOM'S HOMEMADE NOODLES WITH CHICKEN

4-5 lbs. chicken parts (legs, breasts, thighs, wings)
3 large eggs, beaten
3 Tbsps. milk
1/2 tsp. baking powder, sifted with 1 cup flour
Flour enough to make stiff dough

In large pot, cover chicken parts with about 3 quarts water; bring to boil; cook until chicken is tender, about an hour. While chicken cooks, make noodle dough as follows: In bowl, mix well eggs and milk. Add cup flour; with rolling pin, roll out dough until very thin; cover top with flour. Carefully, roll dough back up into a long, thin, cigar-shaped roll. When finished, cut dough into very thin slices forming little thin circles. As they are cut, unroll into strips; lay each on floured surface to dry for about 10 minutes. Take chicken from pot with broth; cool. Bring broth to boil; drop noodles in 1-2 at a time; stir while adding noodles. Cook noodles in broth over low heat about 35-45 minutes; stir often to keep noodles from sticking to bottom of pot. Taste for doneness. When done; bone chicken; add to broth; stir.
Serves 8-10.

"This recipe is given in honor of my Mother who gave it to me many years ago when I was first learning how to cook. It is simple to prepare, delicious on Day One and tastes even better on Days Two and Three!"

Don Van Eynde, San Antonio, Texas

PATRIZIO'S GRILLED CHICKEN

8 large red tip lettuce leaves
6 chicken breasts, boned & skinned
Salt & pepper to taste
1 head Romaine lettuce, rinsed & coarsely chopped
½ head iceberg lettuce, rinsed & coarsely chopped

1 (10 count) can artichoke hearts, drained & quartered
8 strips bacon, cooked crisp & chopped
½ cup slivered almonds, toasted
8 Roma tomatoes, cut in ½-inch pieces

8 stalks hearts of palm, diagonally cut
3 ozs. fresh Romano cheese, grated
4 sprigs fresh basil, chopped
Romano cheese for garnish
Basil sprigs for garnish

Line 4 plates with red leaf lettuce; chill. Season chicken; brush with vinaigrette (below) on both sides; grill over hot coals 4 minutes each side or until done. Cool 5 minutes; cut into chunks. In large bowl, toss together all ingredients with vinaigrette. Arrange on chilled plates; garnish. Excellent Light Entree!

Serves 4.

PATRIZIO'S VINAIGRETTE

1 clove garlic
3 Tbsps. Dijon mustard
2 Tbsps. lemon juice
6 Tbsps. Balsamic vinegar

1 tsp. salt
¼ tsp. pepper
1 Tbsp. fresh basil
1 Tbsp. fresh oregano

⅓ cup extra virgin olive oil
¾ cup safflower oil

In blender, mix first 8 ingredients while gradually adding oils. Blend until thick. Wonderful on green salads too!

Yields about 1½ cups.

Chef Steve Valenti, PATRIZIO'S RESTAURANT, Dallas, Texas

PATRIZIO'S has been named one of Dallas's top ten restaurants and is a great place to dine!

TEXAS FESTIVAL:
The Spinach Festival is held each year in November in Crystal City, the Spinach Capitol of the World and home to a larger than life statue of Pop-Eye the Sailor Man!

LUCINDA'S AFTER CHRISTMAS CASSEROLE

3 Tbsps. green pepper, chopped
3 Tbsps. green onions & tops, chopped
½ cup celery, chopped
2 Tbsps. onion, chopped
1 stick butter, melted

1 (10¾ oz.) can cream of mushroom soup
1 (16 oz.) carton sour cream
1 cup Parmesan cheese, grated
3 Tbsps. fresh parsley, chopped
4 cups turkey, cooked & chopped

1 (8 oz.) can sliced mushrooms, drained
2 (6 oz.) jars artichoke hearts, drained
Dash of Worcestershire & Tabasco
Salt & pepper to taste

In skillet, saute first 4 ingredients in butter; add rest of ingredients; mix. Pour into greased 3-quart casserole; bake at 350° for 45 minutes. This Recipe is Great for Using Leftover Turkey!
Serves 8.

Lucinda H. Presley, Palestine, Texas

WONDERFUL TURKEY ENCHILADAS

2 Tbsps. salad oil, heated
2 (4 oz.) cans green chilies, rinsed, seeded, & chopped
1 large clove garlic, minced
1 (12 oz.) can tomatoes, drained & ½ cup juice reserved

2 cups onion, chopped
Salt to taste
½ tsp. oregano
3 cups turkey, cooked & shredded
1 (16 oz.) carton sour cream

2 cups Cheddar cheese, grated
⅓-½ cup salad oil
15 corn tortillas

To make sauce, saute chilies and garlic in 2 tablespoons oil. Add tomatoes, juice, and next 3 ingredients; simmer, uncovered, until thick, about 30 minutes. Separately, combine next 3 ingredients. Heat oil; dip tortillas in oil until each is limp; drain on paper towels. Fill tortillas with turkey mixture; roll up; place side by side seam side down in skillet; cover with chili sauce; cook until heated through, about 6-8 minutes. Excellent!
Serves 15.

Elma Cornelius McWhorter, Palestine, Texas

TEXAS FESTIVAL:
The Davey Dogwood Park, near Palestine, is a featured area during the annual Texas Dogwood Trails held from March to early April.

STUFFED CORNISH HENS WITH CHARLOTTE'S RICE

¼ cup raisins, soaked over-
night in ½ cup sauterne
¼ cup margarine, melted
1 large onion, chopped &
divided to measure ¼ cup
& ¾ cup
2 cups cornbread

½ tsp. salt
½ tsp. pepper
¼ tsp. poultry seasoning
2 eggs, beaten
1 cup pecans, chopped
¼ cup margarine, melted
4 Cornish hens

¼ cup margarine, melted
1 cup wild or brown rice,
uncooked
¼ cup margarine, melted
1 lb. fresh mushrooms, sliced
½ cup margarine, melted

Saute until tender ¼-cup onions in ¼-cup margarine; stir often. In bowl, combine sauteed onion and cornbread. Add raisins, salt, and next 4 ingredients; mix well. Brush hens' cavities with ¼-cup margarine; stuff hens with dressing. Place on rack in shallow baking pan; bake at 350° an hour or until hens are tender; baste every 15 minutes. Saute ¾-cup onions in ¼-cup margarine; add onions to rice; cook per rice package's directions. Saute mushrooms in ½-cup margarine; stir often. Stir into rice; add more water, if needed; cover; cook 15 minutes or until rice is tender and water absorbed. Split hens; serve immediately with rice on the side. Great!
Serves 8.

Charlotte Webberman, Dallas, Texas

DOVES ALFRED

12-16 doves, split down the
back
¼ cup Burgundy wine
5 ozs. currant jelly

¼ cup barbecue sauce
(page 130)
¼ cup orange juice
1 tsp. orange rind, finely grated

1 stick butter
1 tsp. arrowroot
Watercress & orange slices
for garnish

In broiler pan, place doves, breasts down. In pan over medium heat, combine well next 6 ingredients; add arrowroot. Pour over birds; broil on top rack in oven for 10 minutes or until birds are brown; baste several times. Turn over birds; brush well with sauce; broil 10 minutes more or until crisp and brown; baste often. Remove to hot platter; spoon sauce over doves; garnish.
Serves 6-8.

"I don't know who Alfred is, but Hap Perry and his father, John, guarantee that DOVES ALFRED is the best dove recipe known!"

Mike Hughes, Ingram, Texas

TEXAS VENISON CHILI

2 lbs. venison, coarsely ground
1 large onion, chopped
2 cloves garlic, minced
1/4 cup vegetable oil

2 (10 oz.) cans tomatoes with
    chilies
1 tsp. paprika
1 tsp. salt

1 tsp. cumin
Beef bouillon, beer, or water,
    as needed to cover meat

In Dutch oven, brown first 3 ingredients in oil. Add next 4 ingredients and enough liquid (your choice) to cover all. Cover; simmer over low heat for 1½-2 hours. For thicker chili, mix (1 Tbsp.) flour and (2 Tbsps.) cold water; add to chili; cook a few minutes more.
Serves 6-8.

VENISON STROGANOFF

2½ lbs. venison steak, tendons
    removed, & cut in thin strips
1/2 cup flour, mixed with 1 tsp.
    salt & 1/2 tsp. pepper
1 stick butter, melted

1 onion, chopped
2 cups beef bouillon
8 ozs. mushrooms, sliced
1/2 stick butter
1/2 cup sour cream

1/4 cup tomato paste
1 tsp. Worcestershire sauce
Rice or noodles, cooked per
    pkg.'s directions
Parsley, chopped for garnish

Coat meat with flour. In skillet, slowly brown meat in butter. When brown all over, add onions; cook 2 minutes. Slowly, add bouillon; scrape bottom of skillet to loosen browned particles. Cover; simmer over low heat until meat is tender, about 50 minutes. Separately, saute mushrooms in 1/2 stick butter; add to tender meat. In bowl, combine next 3 ingredients; add to meat; cook 5 minutes more. Serve over rice. Super!
Serves 8.

Mike Hughes, BROKEN ARROW RANCH, Ingram, Texas

Mike owns BROKEN ARROW RANCH which specializes in the harvesting of wild game, primarily deer, for sale to restaurants in the United States and abroad. His products may also be obtained by individuals through mail order!

TEXAS FACT:
Texas' premier wild game animal is the white-tailed deer which is found almost statewide. They have the densest population in the Hill Country of Central Texas where they live in greater numbers than anywhere else in the United States!

135

ABSOLUTE BEST BAKED CATFISH

1 cup fresh Parmesan cheese,
  grated
1/2 cup flour
1/4 tsp. seasoned salt

1/2 tsp. black pepper
1 tsp. paprika
1 egg beaten
1/2 cup milk

6 catfish fillets
1/4 cup butter, melted
1 clove garlic, crushed
Paprika & black pepper

Mix well first 5 ingredients. Separately, mix well egg and milk. Dip fish in egg mixture; dredge in flour mixture. Put fish in greased 9x13-inch baking dish. Saute garlic in butter for 2-3 minutes; drizzle over fish; sprinkle with paprika and pepper; bake at 350° for 40 minutes or until fish flakes. Excellent!
Serves 6.

GRILLED CATFISH WITH AVOCADO MAYONNAISE

1 Tbsp. garlic, minced
2 tsps. basil, minced
1 cup safflower oil
6 catfish fillets
1 ripe avocado, pitted

1 Tbsp. lime juice
1/2 tsp. salt
1 Tbsp. garlic, minced
2 tsps. basil, minced
2 tsps. Balsamic vinegar

1 cup mayonnaise
1 tsp. Dijon mustard
Salt & pepper to taste

To make marinade, mix well first 3 ingredients; marinate fish an hour. To make mayonnaise, puree next 3 ingredients in blender. In saucepan, simmer garlic and basil in vinegar until almost evaporated. Add to blender; add next 2 ingredients; blend. Heat in top of double boiler while grilling fish. Remove fish from marinade; place on hot greased grill. Grill 4-5 minutes each side; don't overcook! Fish will be white and flaky when done. Season; serve with mayonnaise. Very Texas! Delicious!
Serves 6.

Susan Teeple Auler, FALL CREEK VINEYARDS, Austin, Texas

TEXAS FESTIVAL:
Winners of the Lake Meredith Walleye Fishing Tournament are announced at the annual World's Largest Fish Fry held in Borger the first Saturday in June. This famous fish fry features tons of fish served with french fries and cole slaw!

OLD MEXICO FISH FILLETS

2 Tbsps. butter, melted
8 fresh mushrooms, sliced
1 Bermuda onion, sliced
1 carrot, chopped
4 medium tomatoes, coarsely chopped
2 Tbsps. chives, chopped
1½ Tbsps. basil
1 clove garlic, minced
3 green onions & tops, sliced
Salt & pepper to taste
4 fish fillets (your choice!)

Saute mushrooms in butter for 3 minutes; add next 8 ingredients; simmer, covered, for 10-12 minutes. Put fish in greased 1½-quart casserole; pour sauce over fish; bake at 350° for 20-30 minutes or until fish is white and flaky. Easy, Quick, and Good!!
Serves 4. (Easily doubled)

CRAB SUPPER PIE

1 9-inch pastry shell, pricked & baked at 450° 6-8 minutes
8 ozs. lump crab meat, in pieces
4 ozs. shrimp, shelled & cleaned
2½ Tbsps. vermouth
2½ Tbsps. onion, minced
¼ cup butter, melted
Salt & pepper to taste
½ tsp. paprika
1¼ cups heavy cream
⅓ cup Swiss cheese, grated
4 eggs, slightly beaten
Fresh parsley for garnish

Marinate crab meat and shrimp in vermouth for 1-3 hours; drain. Saute onion in butter until soft; add crab/shrimp; cook 3-5 minutes; add next 5 ingredients; stir. Pour into pie shell; bake in upper ⅓ of oven at 375° for 40-45 minutes or until set. Remove; let stand 10 minutes. Wonderful!
Yields 6-8 slices.

Ken Ridgway, Austin, Texas

REAL TEXAS FOLK'S FACT:
Real Texas Folk know that if the proportion of cultivated land in Texas were the same as that in Illinois, the value of Texas crops would equal that of the combined totals of the other 49 states in the union!!

HANGTOWN FRY

½ lb. bacon, cut in large
   pieces, fried crisp, &
   drained
2 Tbsps. butter, melted

12 medium oysters
Flour for breading
1 egg, slightly beaten
1 cup plain bread crumbs

6 eggs, lightly beaten
Salt & pepper to taste

Dip each oyster in flour, egg, then bread crumbs (in that order); fry in skillet with butter until golden brown. Add eggs; cook until set, stirring gently. Top with bacon; heat; season. Serve immediately. Wonderful light supper with salad and garlic bread! Excellent!
Serves 4.

RARE COLLECTION COOKBOOK, The Junior League of Galveston County, Texas

BEST FARMER'S SEAFOOD BOIL

1 gallon water
2 (3 oz.) pkgs. crab/shrimp
   boil
¼ cup salt

3 russet potatoes, unpared
   & quartered
1 link pork sausage, cut in
   1½-inch pieces

4 onions, quartered
2 lbs. headless shrimp
3 ears corn, each cut in thirds

In pot, bring first 3 ingredients to a boil; add potatoes; boil 10 minutes; add sausage and onions; boil 5 minutes; add shrimp and corn; boil 5 minutes. Drain; serve with crusty bread and green salad. Texas Tasty!
Serves 6.

Donna Spaar, Marble Falls, Texas

TEXAS NOTABLE:
John A. "Jack" Johnson, a native of Galveston, was the first African-American to hold the title of World Heavyweight Boxing Champion. Johnson claimed the title after defeating Tommy Burns in 1908 and became the undisputed Champion in 1910 by knocking out James J. Jeffries. Much of Johnson's adult life was chronicled in the award winning Broadway play THE GREAT WHITE HOPE.

TEXAS FACT:
Two Texas towns, Goliad in Southeast Texas, and Mobeetie, have historical markers on their "hanging trees," which were used, on occasion, when dispensing frontier justice!

AUSTIN CITY SHRIMP

½ cup margarine, melted
1½ cups raw shrimp, shelled, cleaned, & cut in ½-inch pieces
½ cup onion, chopped

8 ozs. fresh mushrooms, sliced
2 Tbsps. lemon juice
1 Tbsp. Worcestershire sauce
2 Tbsps. flour
Salt & pepper to taste

8 ozs. sour cream
Parsley & paprika for garnish
3 cups cooked rice or 4-6 slices toast

In margarine, saute shrimp and onion; stir until shrimp are almost tender, about 5 minutes; add next 3 ingredients; cook 5 minutes; remove from heat. Stir in flour; season; add sour cream; cook over low heat five minutes; do NOT boil! Serve, garnished, over rice or hot, buttered toast. *Serves 4-6.*

Ken Ridgway, Austin, Texas

FRIED SHRIMP PECAN

2 cups flour
¼ tsp. cinnamon
2 tsps. baking powder
¼ tsp. salt
3 Tbsps. brown sugar
1¼ cups water

2 tsps. cornstarch
¾ cup water
3 Tbsps. brown sugar
¼ tsp. soy sauce
2 Tbsps. vinegar
Pinch of cayenne pepper

Pinch of salt
2 lbs. jumbo shrimp, peeled, cleaned, & tails left intact
2½ cups pecans, chopped
Oil, heated to 375° for frying

To make batter, sift together first 4 ingredients; stir in sugar; make well in center of dry ingredients; slowly pour 1¼ cups water into well; stir to blend until smooth and thick. Separately, make sauce in small saucepan by stirring cornstarch into ¾-cup water until dissolved; add next 5 ingredients; bring to boil; boil 1 minute to thicken; transfer to serving dish; keep warm. Holding shrimp by tails, dip each in batter, in pecans; then, quickly and gently into oil. Cook for about 2 minutes or until golden; drain. Serve hot with sauce. A Marvelous Main Dish! *Serves 6-8.*

Judy Sneed, Temple, Texas

TEXAS PLACE:
Temple, located in East Texas, is one of the Southwest's leading medical centers and home to Texas A&M University School of Medicine. Temple is also home to the Czech Heritage Museum which highlights Czech contributions to the ethnic diversity of Texas and the Railroad and Pioneer Museum which is devoted to the early pioneer and railroad days in Texas.

MARVELOUS SHRIMP AND PASTA

6-8 ozs. spinach noodles,
   cooked per pkg.'s directions
2 lbs. shrimp, peeled &
   cleaned
1 stick butter, melted
1 cup sour cream

1 (10¾ oz.) can cream of
   mushroom soup
1 cup mayonnaise
1 (8 oz.) can sliced
   mushrooms, drained

1 Tbsp. chives or green onion
   & top, chopped
½ tsp. Dijon mustard
¼ cup sherry
½ cup sharp cheese, grated

In skillet, saute shrimp in butter until pink and tender, about 3-5 minutes. Line buttered casserole with noodles; cover noodles with shrimp. Make sauce by combining sour cream and next 4 ingredients; add mustard and sherry; pour over shrimp; sprinkle cheese over all. Bake at 350° for 30 minutes. Super Easy and Good!
Serves 6-8. (Easily doubled or halved)

Leslie Melson, Dallas, Texas

REAL TEXAS PEEL 'EM AND EAT 'EM SHRIMP

6-8 lbs. large shrimp, unpeeled
2 tsps. salt
2 tsps. black pepper
1 tsp. cayenne pepper

¾ cup salad oil
3 cups onion, chopped
2 cloves garlic, minced
3 cups celery, chopped

3 cups bell pepper, chopped
½ cup green onions & tops,
   chopped
½ cup fresh parsley, chopped

Over medium heat, saute shrimp with next 4 ingredients until shrimp are reddish pink; add next 4 ingredients; over high heat, cover; bring to boil. Reduce heat; simmer 15-20 minutes; add rest of ingredients; stir. Serve, peel 'em and eat 'em style in the sauce. Serve with rice and French bread to dip in the sauce! Your Family or Guests will be So Happy!
Serves 8-10.

Sue Philps, Beaumont, Texas

TEXAS PLACE:
Beaumont, a major port on Texas' Gulf Coast, came of age in 1901 with the world's first oil gusher at Spindletop. Within the month after Spindletop came in, Beaumont, which had been a village, became a city with a population of 30,000!

SHRIMP A LA WILLIAM FOR FOUR

2 lbs. shrimp (in shells)
½ cup salad oil
½ onion, finely chopped
1 Tbsp. parsley

4 fresh tomatoes, boiled 1-3
minutes, skinned, &
chopped
1 garlic pod

1 tube saffron
1 oz. dry white wine
Salt & pepper to taste

Saute shrimp in oil for about 2 minutes each side. Remove shells. Season to taste; set aside. In same pan, saute onion until golden; add next 3 ingredients; cook 10 minutes. Mix shrimp with tomato sauce and rest of ingredients; let simmer 3 minutes. This Sumptuous Dish is Enhanced when Served with Saffron Rice and White Wine!

William Ardid, CHEZ ARDID RESTAURANT, San Antonio, Texas

CHEZ ARDID is an elegant, family owned restaurant in San Antonio. CHEZ ARDID's owner, William, uses many of his grandmother's recipes. Thus, his sauces and cooking techniques are classically French! CHEZ ARDID has a splendid reputation and is a perennial favorite of Texans everywhere!

SHRIMP AND ARTICHOKES

1 (14 oz.) can artichoke
hearts, drained
1 lb. large shrimp, cooked,
peeled, & cleaned
2 Tbsps. butter, melted

½ lb. fresh mushrooms, sliced
4 Tbsps. butter
4 Tbsps. flour
1 cup plus 2 Tbsps. milk
1 Tbsp. Worcestershire sauce

¼ cup dry white wine
¼ cup Parmesan cheese
Paprika

Arrange artichokes in buttered 2-quart casserole; top with shrimp. In skillet, saute mushrooms in 2 tablespoons butter; pour over shrimp. Separately, in saucepan over medium heat, make white sauce as follows: melt butter; stir in flour; cook 2 minutes; add milk; stir until thickened. Combine sauce with Worcestershire and wine; pour over shrimp mixture. Top with Parmesan and paprika. Bake at 375° for 20-30 minutes or until hot. Excellent! Wonderful over Rice or Pasta! *Serves 4.*

Susan Bagwell, Dallas, Texas

TEXAS FANTASTIC SEAFOOD BOUILLABAISSE

4 Tbsps. margarine, melted	4 Tbsps. parsley, chopped	1 lb. crawfish, peeled
4 Tbsps. olive oil	2 Tbsps. lemon juice	1 lb. fresh shrimp, peeled &
½ cup flour	1 bunch green onions & tops,	cleaned
2 medium onions, chopped	chopped	1 lb. fresh bay scallops
4 ribs celery & tops, chopped	2 bay leaves, crushed	1 lb. fresh fish fillets, cubed
6 cloves garlic, chopped	2½ tsps. garlic salt	1 pt. fresh oysters
6-8 cups chicken stock	½ tsp. thyme	1 lb. crab claws
3 (10 oz.) cans Ro-tel tomatoes	Black & cayenne pepper	
1 cup dry white wine	to taste	

In large, heavy pot, add olive oil to margarine; stir in flour; stirring often, cook over medium heat until light brown in color. Add next 3 ingredients; gradually add stock; add next 9 ingredients; bring to boil; simmer 20 minutes. Add crawfish and shrimp; cook 2 minutes; add scallops and fish; cook 2 minutes; add oysters and crab; cook 3-5 minutes; stir twice; cook 6-8 minutes more or until done. Enjoy!
Serves 16. (Easily halved)

"All you need to enjoy this Texas-sized one dish meal is crusty garlic bread! Everyone loves!"

Linda Sue Barnes, George West, Texas

TEXAS FACT:
Indians were the first Texans! Texas Indians represented four culture groups; Southeastern (Caddoes and Atakapans); Plains (Comanches, Apaches, Lipans, Kiowas, Lipan-Apaches, and Kiowa-Apaches); Puebloan (Jumanos and Tiguas); and Western Gulf (Coahuiltocans and Karankawas). The long, varied imprint of Indians in Texas is reflected in the many Indian place names throughout the state. For example, the Town of Nocona, in North Central Texas, is named for the Comanche Chief Peta Nocona, father of the last Chief of the Comanches, Quanah Parker. Nocona, the town, is known as the Leathergoods Center of the Southwest!!

DESSERTS

HURRY-UP APPLE SKILLET CAKE

1½ cups flour
1 cup sugar
Pinch of salt
1 tsp. baking soda

2 apples, peeled & thinly
*   sliced*
½ cup buttermilk
¾ cup vegetable oil

1 egg, lightly beaten
1 tsp. vanilla
1 cup pecans, chopped
1 cup heavy cream, whipped

Sift together first 4 ingredients; add next 6 ingredients; mix well; pour into greased iron skillet. Bake at 350° for 40-50 minutes; serve warm topped with whipped cream. Easy! Good!! An Excellent Coffee Cake Too!

APPLE CRUNCH CAKE SUPREME

2 cups flour
2 cups dark brown sugar,
*   firmly packed*
1 stick unsalted butter, softened
1 cup pecans, toasted &
*   coarsely chopped*

2 tsps. cinnamon
1 tsp. baking soda
½ tsp. salt
1 cup sour cream
2 tsps. vanilla
1 egg, beaten

2½ cups apples, pared, cored,
*   & chopped (about 2 large*
*   apples)*
Powdered sugar

In large bowl, mix until coarse and crumbly first 3 ingredients; stir in pecans; press 2½ cups of mixture into 3-quart oblong baking dish. To rest of pecan mixture, add next 7 ingredients; mix well. Pour on top of crust; bake 50-55 minutes or until cake tester comes out clean. Cool 10 minutes; sprinkle with powdered sugar. Excellent! A Wonderful End to Any Meal!!

Recipe From The Kitchen of Anne Lindsey Greer, Award Winning Author Of
CUISINE OF THE AMERICAN SOUTHWEST And Other Cookbooks

REAL TEXAS FOLK'S FACT:
Real Texas Folk know that Texas owns everything north of the Rio Grande River as well as the river itself, which is the only dusty river in the world and the only one with the possible exception of Texas' Trinity River which is navigable for pedestrians and most four-legged varmints!

BLUEBERRY POUND CAKE

1 pkg. yellow butter cake mix
1 (3½ oz.) pkg. instant
  vanilla pudding
1 (8 oz.) pkg. cream cheese

4 eggs
½ cup vegetable oil
1 tsp. vanilla

1 (15 oz.) can blueberries,
  drained & rinsed
Powdered sugar

In large bowl, mix well first 3 ingredients; beat in eggs, one at a time. Add oil and vanilla; fold in berries; pour into greased, floured Bundt pan; bake at 350° for 1 hour or tests done. Let stand in pan 10 minutes; remove; sprinkle with sugar. Very Good!

Bernice Spears, Lubbock, Texas

GRANDMA JOHNSON'S BANANA CAKE

1¾ cups sugar
1 cup butter
2 large eggs
4 large bananas, mashed
½ cup sour milk*

1 Tbsp. vanilla extract
3 cups flour
2 tsps. baking soda
¾ tsp. salt
⅓ cup butter, softened

Pinch of salt
3 cups powdered sugar
¼ cup milk
2 tsps. vanilla

Preheat oven to 350°. Cream first 3 ingredients well; add next 3 ingredients. (*To make sour milk, add ½ teaspoon vinegar to milk; let sit for 5 minutes.) Separately, combine next 3 ingredients; stir into banana mixture until well mixed. Do not beat. Pour into greased and floured 9x13-inch <u>aluminum</u> pan; reduce oven heat to 325°; bake for 30-40 minutes or until toothpick/tester inserted comes out clean. To make frosting, cream butter, salt and 1 cup sugar until fluffy; add rest of sugar and milk. Blend until smooth; add vanilla. Frost cooled cake, both sides and top. Cake will be very moist, heavy, and delicious!

Marty Bennett, Houston, Texas

TEXAS PLACE:
Palo Duro Canyon State Park, with 15,103 acres, is Texas' largest state park. An historical marker in the park, which is located near Canyon, Texas, in the Panhandle Region, cites the last great Indian battle fought in Texas. The Park is home to the Pioneer Amphitheater which provides the setting for TEXAS, a spectacular outdoor drama, presented nightly (except Sundays) from late June through late August.

LEE'S INCREDIBLE SUGAR POUND CAKE

1 stick butter
1 cup vegetable shortening
1 cup sugar
16 ozs. light brown sugar
1½ tsps. vanilla
5 eggs

3⅓ cups cake flour, sifted
½ tsp. baking powder
1 tsp. salt
1 cup evaporated milk
1 cup coconut
1 cup pecans, chopped

⅓ cup butter, melted
1 cup light brown sugar, firmly packed
¼ cup evaporated milk
1 tsp. vanilla

Cream butter and shortening; gradually, add sugars; beat until fluffy; blend in vanilla. Add eggs, one at a time; beat after each addition. Sift together next 3 ingredients; add to creamed mixture, alternating with milk; fold in coconut and nuts. Pour into well geased and floured tube pan; bake at 325° for 1 hour 45 minutes or tests done; cool. To make glaze, in saucepan, blend sugar with butter; add milk; bring to boil; cook 2 minutes; remove from heat; cool; add vanilla; beat until creamy. Frost cooled cake. Good!

Lee Kennedy, Mesquite, Texas

GRANDMOTHER'S POUND CAKE

2 sticks butter, softened
1⅔ cups sugar

5 eggs
2 cups flour, sifted

1 tsp. vanilla
Non-stick vegetable spray

Cream butter and sugar; beat until fluffy; add flour, a little at a time, alternating with eggs; end with flour; add vanilla. Bake in bundt or tube pan that has been sprayed <u>well</u> with vegetable spray. Bake at 325° for an hour. A Southern Treat!

"I have been married almost 50 years and have made this cake for my family all my married life!"

Elizabeth Findling, San Antonio, Texas

TEXAS FACT:
A Texan, A.J. Foyt, Jr., of Houston has won the premier automobile race, the Indianapolis 500, more than any other professional race car driver! Foyt has won four times, in 1961, 1964, 1967, and 1970.

CHOCOLATE BLACKBERRY WINE CAKE

1 (18.5 oz.) pkg. chocolate cake mix
1 (3 oz.) pkg. blackberry gelatin
4 eggs
½ cup cooking oil
1 cup blackberry wine (Manischewitz is best!)
½ cup pecans, chopped
1 stick butter, melted
½ cup blackberry wine
1 cup powdered sugar

Combine first 2 ingredients; with electric mixer on low, beat in next 3 ingredients until batter is moist; beat on medium speed until batter is smooth. Sprinkle pecans into greased, heavily floured bundt pan; pour in batter; bake at 325° for 45-50 minutes or tests done. In saucepan, combine butter and wine; bring to good boil; stir; remove from heat. While cooked cake is still in bundt pan, cover cake with ½ wine mixture; cool cake 30 minutes; turn onto cake plate. Stir sugar into rest of wine mixture until mixture is thickened and smooth; pour over cake. Different and Good!

James Clark, Dallas, Texas

CHOCOLATE ITALIAN CREAM CAKE

1 stick butter, softened
½ cup Crisco
2 cups sugar
5 eggs, separated
1 tsp. baking soda
2 cups flour
¼ cup cocoa
1 cup buttermilk
1 cup coconut
1 tsp. vanilla
1 cup pecans, chopped
1 stick butter, softened
1 (8 oz.) pkg. cream cheese, room temperature
1 tsp. vanilla
1 (16 oz.) box powdered sugar
¼ cup cocoa
½ cup pecans, chopped

Cream first 3 ingredients; add yolks, one at a time; beat after each addition. Sift together next 3 ingredients; add to egg mixture, alternating with buttermilk (begin and end with dry ingredients). Stir in coconut, vanilla, and nuts. Beat egg whites stiff; fold into batter. Bake at 325° in 3 greased and floured 8-inch round cake pans for 25-30 minutes; cool cake to frost. To make frosting, cream butter and cheese; add vanilla; sift together sugar and cocoa; beat, a little at a time, into butter mixture; add nuts; spread on cooled cakes; stack; smooth frosting over all. Elegant!

Doris Krajca, Ennis, Texas

GREAT FLAVORS' CHOCOLATE FUDGE TRUFFLE CAKE

1 (23 oz.) brownie mix
2 Tbsps. water
3 eggs
1 tsp. vanilla
Non-stick vegetable spray

2 (12 oz.) pkgs. semi-sweet
   chocolate chips
2 Tbsps. espresso coffee,
   dissolved in 1/3 cup water
1/2 cup coffee liqueur

1/3 cup sugar
2 cups heavy cream, whipped
1 (6 oz.) pkg. chocolate chips
1/4 cup coffee liqueur

Preheat oven to 350°. In large bowl, mix well first 4 ingredients; spray 11x15-inch jelly roll pan well with vegetable spray; pour batter into pan; bake for 10 minutes; turn cake onto flat surface; cool. Make filling as follows: Melt chocolate chips with next 3 ingredients in microwave (or conventionally); cool; fold in cream. Cut cake in 2 8-inch rounds and 2 strips; only 1 round will be perfect; other will have to be pieced together. In 8-inch spring form pan, piece together imperfect round on pan's bottom; place strips around pan's inside edges; piece together, if necessary, and press with fingers to fill any holes. Pour filling into cake; top with other 8-inch round; chill 3-4 hours. To make glaze, melt rest of ingredients in microwave (or conventionally). Remove cake from pan; spread with glaze; refrigerate until ready to serve. Magnificent and Worth the Little Extra Effort!!
Serves 12.

Sherry Ferguson, GREAT FLAVORS OF TEXAS

TEXAS FACT AND TREASURE:
Big Spring, Texas, seat of Howard County in West Texas, is named for the huge natural spring on Sulphur Draw that for centuries watered buffalo, antelope, wild mustangs, and the Comanche and Shawnee Indians of the Great Plains. The spring, today, is at the center of a city park.

Big Spring's Heritage Museum has the largest collection in the world of Henry W. Caylor's paintings. Caylor lived and worked in Big Spring for 40 years, and many of his marvelous western scenes were commissioned by wealthy ranchers.

MICHAEL'S BIRTHDAY CAKE

2 cups flour
1⅓ cups sugar
3 tsps. baking pwder
½ tsp. salt
½ cup salad oil
8 medium egg yolks, unbeaten

¾ cups cold water
2 tsps. vanilla _or_ almond
   extract
8 medium egg whites, stiffly
   beaten with ½ tsp. cream
   of tartar

4 ozs. unsweetened chocolate,
   shaved
18 ozs. (1 small & 1 large
   pkg.) Nestle's chocolate
   chips
1½ pts. (24 ozs.) sour cream

Mix well first 4 ingredients; make a well in center of ingredients; add oil, yolks, water, and extract; beat until smooth. Gradually, pour yolk mixture over egg whites, and gently fold in with shaved chocolate until just blended. DO NOT STIR! Pour into lightly greased tube pan; bake at 325° for 55 minutes; cake will be firm yet springy; invert until cool. To make icing, melt chips over very low heat; remove from burner; stir until smooth; add sour cream; blend well. Spread on cake immediately; refrigerate. Wonderful!

"Both my son's grandmothers contributed to this cake — one the cake recipe and the other the sour cream icing! Michael has had this special cake made on his birthday for many birthday celebrations!"

Carolann Gerescher, San Antonio, Texas

CHOCOLATE MARSHMALLOW CREAM CAKE

1 cup butter, softened
4 eggs
2 cups sugar
1½ cups flour

⅓ cup cocoa
1 tsp. vanilla extract
1 cup nuts, chopped
1 (8 oz.) jar marshmallow cream

½ cup butter, softened
6 Tbsps. milk
⅓ cup cocoa
1 (16 oz.) box powdered sugar

Beat butter until creamy; add eggs, one at a time; beat well after each addition. Add next 5 ingredients; mix well; pour into greased and floured 9x13-inch pan; spread evenly; bake at 350° for 35-40 minutes or tests done. When done; spread marshmallow cream over hot cake; let cool 20 minutes. To make frosting, combine rest of ingredients; spread over cake; swirl through marshmallow cream for marbled look! Fantastic!

Joy E. Levens, San Antonio, Texas

EASY N' DELICIOUS EGGNOG CAKE

1 Angel Food Cake
1 stick butter
2 cups powdered sugar, sifted
2 egg yolks
1 tsp. vanilla
2 Tbsps. sherry
2 Tbsps. bourbon
5 Tbsps. coffee creamer
1½ cups heavy cream, whipped
Nutmeg for sprinkling

With serrated knife, cut cake into 4 layers. Cream butter with sugar until fluffy. Blend in yolks, one at a time; stir in next 4 ingredients; spread on tops of each layer; reassemble cake. Ice with whipped cream; top with nutmeg. Refrigerate 6 hours or more before serving. Delightful!!
Serves 12.

Sandy Thompson, San Antonio, Texas

ITALIAN CREAM CAKE

1 stick butter, softened
½ cup vegetable oil
2 cups sugar
5 eggs, separated
2 cups flour
1 tsp. baking soda
1 cup buttermilk
1 tsp. vanilla
1 cup coconut
½ cup pecans, chopped
1 stick butter, softened
1 (8 oz.) pkg. cream cheese
1 (16 oz.) box powdered sugar, sifted
1 tsp. vanilla
1 cup pecans, chopped

With electric mixer, cream first 3 ingredients; add yolks, one at a time; beat after each addition. Sift flour and soda together; add to egg mixture, alternating with buttermilk; mix in next 3 ingredients. Separately, beat egg whites stiff; fold into batter; pour into 3 greased 9-inch round cake pans; bake at 350° for 20-25 minutes or tests done; cool. To make frosting, cream stick butter and cream cheese; add sugar and vanilla; beat until smooth; frost cooled cake; stack in 3 layers; top with pecans. Excellent!

Lee Kennedy, Mesquite, Texas

TEXAS FACT:
Mesquite, Texas, is home to the Mesquite Championship Rodeo, which has performances every Friday and Saturday night from April through September. This rodeo began in 1958 as an experiment with an ongoing rodeo format and has become a very successful attraction!

HOLIDAY PUMPKIN CAKE

4 eggs
2 cups sugar
2 cups pumpkin
1½ cups oil
2 cups flour

1 tsp. salt
2 tsps. baking powder
2 tsps. baking soda
2 tsps. cinnamon
1½ cups pecans, chopped

1 (8 oz.) pkg. cream cheese, softened
½ stick margarine
1 (16 oz.) pkg. powdered sugar
½ cup pecans, chopped

Cream first 4 ingredients until smooth. Sift together next 5 ingredients; mix in nuts; add dry mixture to creamed mixture, a little at a time. Mix well after each addition; pour batter into greased bundt pan; bake at 350° for 45-55 minutes; turn onto plate to cool. To make icing, combine cheese, margarine, and sugar; stir in nuts; ice cake. Enjoy!

Jean Williams, Wimberley, Texas

When in Wimberley, visit JEAN'S ANTIQUES, GIFTS, AND BOUTIQUE, a super shop that also has neat gourmet items!

DELICIOUS CHOCOLATE ROLL

5 eggs, separated
1 cup sugar
3 Tbsps. flour
3 Tbsps. cocoa

Powdered sugar
1 cup heavy cream, whipped
1 cup sugar
3 Tbsps. flour

3 Tbsps. cocoa
1 stick margarine
1 cup warm water
1 tsp. vanilla

In bowl, beat yolks; add sugar; beat well; mix in flour and cocoa. Separately, beat egg whites stiff; fold into yolk mixture. Pour batter into greased and floured 9x11-inch pan; bake at 350° for 25-30 minutes; cool 5 minutes; turn cake onto wax paper sprinkled with powdered sugar; let cake cool. Cover with whipped cream; roll cake up like jelly roll; chill 3-4 hours. Make sauce by combining rest of ingredients; cook over low heat until thick; stir often. Slice cake; top with sauce.

Mary Jo Dudley, Wichita Falls, Texas

TEXAS NOTABLE:
Larry McMurtry, the noted author, is a native of Wichita Falls. The son and grandson of cattlemen, he understands the romantic myths and harsh realities of cowboy life. His novels include THE LAST PICTURE SHOW, TERMS OF ENDEARMENT, and LEAVING CHEYENNE.

MANDARIN ORANGE CAKE

1 pkg. yellow cake mix
1 (16 oz.) can mandarin
   oranges with juice
1 cup cooking oil

4 eggs
1 (8 oz.) can crushed
   pineapple with juice
1 (3 oz.) can coconut

1 (3½ oz.) can vanilla instant
   pudding
1 (13 oz.) carton frozen
   whipped topping

In bowl, mix well first 3 ingredients; add eggs, one at a time; beat well after each addition. Pour into 4 greased and floured 9-inch round cake pans. Bake at 350° for 15-20 minutes; cool. To make frosting, mix well rest of ingredients; frost cooled cake; stack. Keep cake refrigerated. The Perfect Summertime Treat!!

Faye Gilmore, Possum Kingdom Lake, Texas

MEXICAN CAKE

2 cups flour
2 cups sugar
2 tsps. baking soda
2 eggs

1 (20 oz.) can crushed
   pineapple with juice
1 (8 oz.) pkg. cream cheese
1 stick margarine

2 cups powdered sugar
1 tsp. vanilla

Mix well first 5 ingredients; bake at 350° in greased and floured 8x12-inch baking pan for 45-50 minutes; cool. Beat until smooth remaining ingredients; frost cooled cake; refrigerate. Delicious and Light Cake that is Perfect after a Hearty Meal!
Yields 12-16 slices.

Daisy Brown, San Antonio, Texas

TEXAS NOTABLE:
James Frank Dobie, born on a ranch in Live Oak County, had a literary and teaching career which was intricately woven into the fabric that is Texas. Dobie loved and understood his hard land and the people who struggled for a living on it. His life's work was to interpret the southwestern heritage in books and articles. THE LONGHORNS was his most popular book. For Dobie, the longhorn represented the strength, vitality, freedom, endurance, and inherent nobility of not only the longhorns but also the men who cared for them. His other works include VAQUERO OF THE BRUSH COUNTRY, CORONADO'S CHILDREN, and APACHE GOLD AND YAQUI SILVER, which contains the treasure stories that Dobie loved so well.

HATTIE'S MAKE AHEAD COCONUT CAKE

1 pkg. butter flavored cake mix, prepared per pkg.'s instructions & cooked in 2 8-inch round pans

16 ozs. sour cream
2 (12 oz.) pkgs. frozen coconut, slightly thawed
2 cups sugar

1 (8 oz.) pkg. frozen whipped topping, thawed

Cool cooked cake; carefully split each layer in half (I use dental floss to split cake layers!). Combine sour cream, coconut, and sugar; reserve 1 cup of mixture for icing; spread remainder over tops of 4 layers; stack. Combine reserved mixture with topping; spread on sides and cake's top. Seal cake in airtight container; refrigerate 3 days before serving. Nothing Better!

Hattie Hasie, Lubbock, Texas

SOUTHWEST SHERRY CAKE

1 pkg. butter flavored cake mix
1 (3½ oz.) pkg. instant vanilla pudding
4 eggs

½ cup vegetable oil
½ cup water
½ cup cream sherry
⅔ cup pecans, chopped
1 cup sugar

1 stick butter
⅓ cup cream sherry
⅓ cup pecans, chopped

Mix well first 6 ingredients; fold in ⅔ cup nuts; pour into greased and lightly floured bundt pan; bake at 325° for 45-60 minutes or tests done. In saucepan, combine rest of ingredients; boil 2-3 minutes; pour over warm cake while cake is still in pan. Let cake remain in pan for at least 1-1½ hours. For a change, substitute amaretto and chopped almonds for cream sherry and pecans. Excellent!

Roberta Searls, San Antonio, Texas

TEXAS FESTIVAL:
Lubbock, the Chrysanthemum Capital of the World, hosts the annual Panhandle South Plains Fair during the last week in September. This fair is one of the largest regional fairs in Texas and draws about 250,000 visitors to its pageants, contests, entertainment, and traditional fair exhibits!

RAINBOW CAKE SPECTACULAR

3 sticks butter, softened
2¼ cups sugar
4 eggs
1 tsp. vanilla extract

1½ tsps. lemon extract
5½ cups cake flour
½ tsp. salt
4½ tsps. baking powder

1 cup plus 2 Tbsps. milk
Red, green, & yellow food coloring
Powdered sugar

With mixer, cream butter; add sugar, a little at a time; beat; add eggs, one at a time; beat 1 minute after each addition; add extracts. Sift flour with next 2 ingredients; add to creamed mixture, 1 cup at a time, alternating with 3-4 tablespoons milk; beat until very smooth. Divide batter into 3 bowls as follows: 3½ cups, add 3-5 drops red food coloring; 2¾ cups, add 3-5 drops green food coloring; 2¼ cups, add yellow food coloring. Using only a greased and floured bundt pan, first pour in red batter; spoon in green batter; spoon in yellow batter; spread each layer very carefully. Bake 1 hour at 325°, then, 20 minutes more at 350°. Cool; turn onto cake rack; sprinkle thickly with sugar. Wonderful!

Claudia Erdmann, Dallas, Texas

LADY'S RUM CAKE

1 cup pecans, chopped
1 (18½ oz.) pkg. yellow cake mix
1 (3¾ oz.) pkg. vanilla instant pudding & pie filling

4 eggs
½ cup cold water
½ cup oil
½ cup dark rum (80 proof)

1 stick butter, melted
¼ cup water
1 cup granulated sugar
½ cup dark rum (80 proof)

Grease and flour bundt or tube pan; sprinkle nuts in bottom of pan. Mix well next 6 ingredients; pour batter over nuts; bake at 325° for 1 hour; cool; turn onto serving plate; prick cake's top. To make glaze, combine butter, water, and sugar in saucepan; boil 5 minutes; stir constantly; stir in rum; drizzle over top and sides of cake. Delicious!

Lady Cleo Bischoff, San Antonio, Texas

TEXAS NOTABLE:
John Howard Griffin, a native of Dallas, has had a varied and prolific literary career. Griffin, a white man, is perhaps best known for his 1961 autobiographical work, BLACK LIKE ME, which relates the story of his experiences traveling through the South disguised as a black man. His other works include MANSFIELD, TEXAS and SCATTERED SHADOWS.

WHITE CHOCOLATE CAKE WITH WHITE CHOCOLATE FROSTING

8 ozs. white chocolate	*2½ cups cake flour, sifted*	*2½ Tbsps. flour*
½ cup water, boiling	*with 1 tsp. baking soda*	*½ cup milk*
2 sticks butter	*1 cup buttermilk*	*2 sticks butter*
2 cups sugar	*1 cup pecans, chopped*	*1 cup sugar*
4 eggs, separated	*1 cup coconut, shredded*	*½ tsp. vanilla*
1 tsp. vanilla	*¾ cup white chocolate*	*Fresh strawberries*

Melt chocolate in water; cool. Cream butter and sugar; add yolks, vanilla, and cooled chocolate; mix well. Add flour, a little at a time; alternate with buttermilk; mix after each addition. Beat egg whites; fold into batter; stir in pecans and coconut. Pour into 3 9-inch greased and floured cake pans; bake at 350° for 40-45 minutes or tests done; cool. To make frosting, combine ¾ cup chocolate, flour, and milk in top of double boiler; cook until <u>very</u> thick; cool. Mix well next 3 ingredients; let stand 30 minutes; add cooled chocolate; whip until creamy. Frost cooled cake; stack. Serve with strawberries. Delicious and Elegant!

Beverly Smith, New Braunfels, Texas

HEAVENLY FROZEN MOCHA CHEESECAKE

1¼ cups chocolate wafer	*1 (8 oz.) pkg. cream cheese*	*2 Tbsps. instant coffee*
cookies (24), crumbled	*14 ozs. sweetened condensed*	*1 tsp. hot water*
¼ cup sugar	*milk*	*1 cup heavy cream, whipped*
¼ cup butter	*⅔ cup chocolate syrup*	*Chocolate shavings*

To make crust combine first 3 ingredients; pat crumbs firmly on bottom and up sides of a 9-inch springform pan or 9x13-inch pan; chill. Beat cheese until fluffy; add next 2 ingredients. Separately, dissolve coffee in water; add to cheese mixture; fold in whipped cream; pour into crust. Cover with foil; freeze 6 hours or until firm. Serve garnished with chocolate shavings. Wonderful!

Serves 12-15.

Jane Ferguson, Fort Worth, Texas

MARVELOUS CHOCOLATE TURTLE CHEESECAKE

2 cups vanilla wafer cookie crumbs
6 Tbsps. butter, melted
1 (14 oz.) bag caramel candy
1 (5 oz.) can evaporated milk
1½ cups pecans, chopped & roasted
2 (8 oz.) pkgs. cream cheese
½ cup sugar
1 Tbsp. vanilla
2 eggs
½ cup semi-sweet chocolate chips, melted
1 cup pecans, chopped for garnish

To make crust, mix well crumbs with butter; press into bottom and sides of greased 8½-inch springform pan; bake 10 minutes at 350°; set aside. To make filling, in saucepan over low heat, combine candy and milk; cook; stir often until candy melts, and mixture is smooth; cool 5 minutes; pour over crust. Do <u>not</u> let candy mixture come quite to edge of crust; top with nuts. Separately, with electric mixer, mix well cheese with next 3 ingredients; add chocolate; mix; pour over pecans; bake at 350° 30 minutes; cool. Refrigerate overnight. Before serving, sprinkle with chopped nuts. *Serves 8-10.*

INCREDIBLE PUMPKIN CHEESECAKE

1¼ cups graham cracker crumbs
⅓ cup sugar
2 Tbsps. butter, softened
16 ozs. cream cheese
¾ cup sugar
1½ Tbsps. flour
Rinds of 1 orange & 1 lemon, grated
2 eggs plus 2 egg yolks
1 cup fresh pumpkin puree
2 tsps. ground cinnamon
16 ozs. sour cream
5 Tbsps. sugar
1 Tbsp. clear vanilla
1 cup walnuts, chopped coarsely & toasted

To make crust, mix well first 3 ingredients; press into 8½-inch lightly greased springform pan; bake 5 minutes at 350°; set aside. To make filling, with electric mixer, combine next 4 ingredients; add eggs and yolks; blend until smooth; stir in pumpkin and cinnamon; pour over crust; cook 40 minutes at 350°. To make topping, combine sour cream, sugar, and vanilla; spread over baked cheesecake; return to oven for 10 minutes more; cool; refrigerate overnight. At serving time, top with walnuts. *Yields 8-10 slices.*

"My Halloween pumpkin forms the basis for this Thanksgiving holiday dessert!"

Ellen Tipton, Houston, Texas

JEANNIE'S BIRTHDAY FUDGE PUDDING

2 eggs, beaten until thick	*1 tsp. vanilla*	*Pinch of salt*
1 cup sugar	*⅛ cup flour*	*1 cup pecans, chopped*
1 stick butter, melted	*2 heaping Tbsps. cocoa*	*Ice cream or whipped cream*

With electric mixer, gradually add sugar to beaten eggs while continuing to beat; mix in next 5 ingredients; stir in nuts with spoon. Pour into greased 8x12-inch pyrex pan; put pan in slightly larger pan; add about 1-inch of hot water; bake at 325° for 45 minutes. To serve, cut in 8 squares, and top with ice cream or whipped cream. Pudding will be crusty on top and gooey inside! Good!
Serves 6-8.

"My sister gave me this recipe, and it's always a hit. In fact, it's probably my family's favorite recipe and is sometimes requested in lieu of birthday cake!"

Helen Fairchild Clement, Native of Houston, Texas

BANANA PUDDING

6-8 bananas, sliced	*2 (2.9 oz.) pkgs. instant*	*12 ozs. Cool Whip*
1 (11 oz.) box vanilla	*vanilla pudding*	*8 ozs. sour cream*
wafers	*4 cups cold milk*	

Layer ½ bananas and ½ cookies in bottom of 11x14-inch pan. Combine pudding and milk; fold in rest of ingredients; pour ½ pudding over bananas in pan; top with rest of cookies and bananas; top with rest of pudding; refrigerate. Delicious And Easy!
Serves 8-10.

Mikey Herndon, Austin, Texas

TEXAS FACT AND TREASURE:
Texas has six main land regions. They are the Coastal Plains, Hill Country (South Central), Basin and Range (Southwest), Great Plains (West), High Plains (Panhandle), and Interior Plains (North Central). Texas' diverse geography is a bonanza for rock and mineral collectors! Some of the stones to be found in Texas are agate, amethyst, granite, cinnabar, and topaz. Texas' state stone is pertrified palmwood.

MAMA'S HOFBRAU BREAD PUDDING WITH WHISKEY SAUCE

4 qts. day old bread, cut in 3/4-inch cubes	2 cups bananas, sliced 1/4-inch thick	1 1/2 cups sugar
1 3/4 cups sugar	3/4 cup raisins	2 sticks butter, melted
3 eggs	1/3 cup butter	2 ozs. Scotch whiskey
2 cups milk	3 Tbsps. & 3/4 tsp. cinnamon	2 eggs, lightly beaten
1/3 cup vanilla	2 3/4 tsps. nutmeg	

Mix 1 1/2 cups sugar with next 3 ingredients; pour over bread; mix well by hand to make sure bread is soaked; add bananas and raisins; mix by hand. Put pudding in 5-quart pan or casserole; smooth top; dot with butter; sprinkle with 1/4 cup sugar, cinnamon and nutmeg; bake at 225° for 1 1/4 hours. To make sauce, in saucepan, combine butter and sugar; stir 2 minutes; reduce heat to low; add scotch slowly; stir constantly until sugar dissolves; stir whiskey mixture into eggs; cook until sauce begins to thicken. To serve, spoon sauce over slightly cooled pudding. A Real Treat!

Serves 18-20 (Easily halved)

MAMA'S HOFBRAU RESTAURANT, San Antonio, Texas

COMPANY BLUEBERRIES AND CREME FRAICHE

2 pints fresh blueberries, rinsed & drained	20 amaretto cookies	2 Tbsps. buttermilk
1/4 cup sugar	1 cup heavy cream, whipped	1 cup sour cream

Sprinkle blueberries with sugar; set aside. Crush cookies between wax paper with rolling pin. In a glass bowl, make creme fraiche by combining rest of ingredients; let mixture stand at room temperature for 2 hours; refrigerate. To serve, in parfait glasses or serving bowl, layer blueberries, creme fraiche, and cookie crumbs; repeat layering 2-3 times. (Creme fraiche may be purchased ready made. If purchased, use 1 pint.) A Wonderful Elegant Dessert!

Serves 4-6.

Paula Lambert, Dallas, Texas

AVOCADO SHERBET WONDERFUL

1½ cups avocado, mashed	*1 cup orange juice*	*2 tsps. lemon peel, grated*
1 cup lemon juice	*2 cups sugar*	*2 cups heavy cream, whipped*

Mix well first 5 ingredients until sugar is totally dissolved; pour into ice cube trays; freeze 30 minutes. Turn sherbet into bowl; stir; fold in cream; pack into plastic container; freeze until firm. A Great Flavor of Texas!
Serves 12.

BLUEBERRY SHERRY ICE CREAM

2 Tbsps. cornstarch	*2 cups fresh <u>or</u> frozen*	*¼ cup creme de cacao*
½ cup sugar	*blueberries*	*½ gallon vanilla ice cream,*
¾ cup water	*½ cup dry sherry*	*softened*

Combine cornstarch and sugar, stir in water and ½ cup blueberries; cook over low heat; stir constantly until thickened. Add remaining blueberries; cool; add rest of ingredients; freeze 8 hours. Outstanding!!
Serves 4-6.

PECOS CANTALOUPE ICE CREAM

1½ cups sugar	*1 (14 oz.) can condensed milk*	*1 large, ripe cantaloupe,*
Pinch of salt	*1 (13 oz.) can evaporated milk*	*pureed in blender*
3 eggs, well beaten	*1 qt. milk*	*Ice cream salt*

Add sugar and salt to eggs; stir in milks; add cantaloupe; put in ice cream freezer; cover; pack with ice and salt; freeze until firm. Another Great Flavor of Texas!
Yields 1 gallon.

FLAVORS COOKBOOK, The Junior League of San Antonio, Texas

All three of the marvelous, unique recipes on this page are guaranteed to please all palates and are shared with you courtesy of the Junior League of San Antonio. The league's cookbook, FLAVORS, is a fantastic one now in its fifth printing! Revenues generated from the sale of FLAVORS go to better the quality of life for the San Antonio Community.

BEST EVER CRANBERRY SHERBET

1 lb. cranberries, boiled in 3 cups water
3 cups sugar
½ (3.9 oz.) pkg. raspberry jello
¾ cup fresh orange juice
¼ cup fresh grapefruit juice
2 egg whites
¼ tsp. salt

Puree cooked cranberries. Separately, mix next 4 ingredients; mix with cranberries; freeze 2 hours. Put sherbet in bowl; beat until fluffy with whites and salt; put in plastic container; freeze. Very Delicious! Super served in dessert glasses with a holiday dinner in place of congealed cranberry salad or relish!
Serves 6.

RUBY RED GRAPEFRUIT SHERBET

2 cups sugar
3 cups water
2 egg whites, stiffly beaten
2 cups ruby red grapefruit juice
½ cup lemon juice

Boil sugar and water to a syrup, about 5 minutes; pour into whites; beat constantly; add juices; freeze 4 hours; beat until smooth; freeze overnight. Delightful!
Makes about 2 quarts.

FRANK LEWIS' ALAMO FRUIT COMPANY, Alamo, Texas

FRESH PEACH ICE CREAM

1 qt. fresh peaches, peeled & diced
2 cups sugar
2 tsps. vanilla
1 qt. half & half, mixed with 1 cup sugar & 1 pt. heavy cream

In blender, mix well peaches and sugar. Combine vanilla with cream mixture; stir in with peaches. Pour into freezer; freeze per freezer's directions. The Creamiest Homemade Ice Cream Ever!
Makes 1 gallon.

Linda Sue Barnes, George West, Texas

ANATOLE'S CHAMPAGNE AND RAISIN ICE CREAM

1 cup raisins	*3 cups cream*	*1¼ cups sugar*
⅔ cup champagne	*1 vanilla bean*	
2 cups milk	*10 egg yolks*	

Marinate raisins in champagne overnight; reserve champagne. In saucepan, bring next 3 ingredients to boil; remove from heat. In top of double boiler, over simmering water, whisk yolks, sugar, ½ reserved champagne, and raisins. Whisk until mixture is 3 times its original volume, about 10-12 minutes; whisk in milk mixture; beat 10 minutes; refrigerate overnight. Remove vanilla bean; freeze in ice cream freezer per freezer's instructions.
Serves 8-10.

Michel Bernard Platz, Chef de Cuisine, ANATOLE HOTEL, Dallas, Texas

ELEGANT CHAMPAGNE MOUSSE

2 cups milk	*1 Tbsp. gelatin, dissolved in*	*1 Tbsp. Grand Marnier*
1 cup sugar	*¼ cup water*	*1 cup heavy cream*
½ tsp. salt	*1 cup pink champagne*	*Fresh strawberries or favorite*
4 eggs, beaten	*1 qt. heavy cream, whipped*	*fresh fruit*

In top of double boiler, heat first 3 ingredients; add eggs; stir until thickened. Remove from burner; stir in gelatin; cool; add champagne; stir until thick. Fold in quart whipped cream; put in plastic container; freeze 8 hours. Before serving, combine Grand Marnier and cream; whip. Spoon mousse in parfait glasses; top with fruit and whipped cream. Grand!
Serves 4-6.

Carolyn Bruce Rose, Dallas, Texas

TEXAS NOTABLE AND PLACE:
Chef Michel Bernard Platz is world renown for his simply elegant cuisine. His kitchen is housed in the magnificent Anatole Hotel which is the largest hotel in the Southwest. The Anatole's marvelous and unique art and antique collections bring great joy to visitors and are two of the finest collections in the United States!

JOHN'S FAVORITE BROWNIE TORTE

1 (15½ oz.) pkg. fudge
  brownie mix
¼ cup water
2 eggs

1 cup pecans, finely chopped
2 cups heavy cream, chilled
½ cup plus 2 Tbsps. brown
  sugar

1 Tbsp. powdered
  instant coffee
1 square semi-sweet
  chocolate, grated

Combine first 4 ingredients; spread in 2 greased and floured 9-inch cake pans; bake 20 minutes at 350°; cool; turn on wire racks. In chilled bowl, beat cream; gradually, add sugar and coffee; beat until stiff; place 1 cake layer on dish; cover with 1 cup cream; top with second layer; frost top with rest of cream; top with chocolate; chill 4 hours before serving. Elegant Results!
Serves 10-12.

MEXICAN CREAM TORTE OLE

1¾ cups vanilla wafer crumbs
¼ cup butter, melted
3 pts. (48 ozs.) chocolate ice
  cream

1 (12 oz.) jar Smucker's
  chocolate fudge syrup
1½ pints orange sherbet

2 cups peanut brittle,
  crushed
Fresh mint sprigs for garnish

Mix well crumbs and butter; press into bottom of 9-inch springform pan; bake at 350° 8 minutes; cool; refrigerate. Layer ½ chocolate ice cream over crust; cover with ½ chocolate syrup; freeze. Top frozen syrup with orange sherbet; top with syrup; top syrup with chocolate ice cream; sprinkle candy over top; freeze 6 hours or overnight. Serve garnished. Makes a Lovely Presentation.
Serves 10-12.

SUPREME OREO SMUSH

1 stick margarine
1 (19 oz.) pkg. Oreos,
  crushed

½ gallon vanilla ice cream,
  softened

2 (12 oz.) jars Smucker's
  fudge sauce
1 (8 oz.) carton Cool Whip

Melt margarine in 9x13-inch pan. Mix crumbs with margarine; reserve a few crumbs. Form crust in pan. Spread ice cream over crust; add layer of fudge sauce. Top with Cool Whip; sprinkle with remaining crumbs. Keep frozen until ready to serve. A Winner!
Serves 16-18.

Melinda Wright, McAllen, Texas

FAVORITE LEMON CLOUD

2 cups flour	1½ cups lemon juice	1 cup sugar
2 Tbsps. sugar	1 lemon rind, grated	Pinch of salt
1 cup butter	1 envelope unflavored gelatin,	1 cup heavy cream, whipped
8 egg yolks, beaten	softened in ⅔ cup water	3½ ozs. coconut
1 cup sugar	8 egg whites	Juice of 1 orange & rind, grated

To make crust, mix first 2 ingredients; cut in butter; press into 9x13-inch pan. In top of double boiler, mix next 4 ingredients; add gelatin; cook over medium heat until mixture coats spoon; cool. Beat whites with sugar and salt until stiff; fold into cooled custard; pour into crust; top with cream. Mix rest of ingredients; spoon onto paper towels to absorb juice; sprinkle rind and coconut over whipped cream; refrigerate overnight. Good!
Serves 12.

"This is a family favorite and light, airy, and sinfully delicious!"

Genie Calgaard, San Antonio, Texas

STRAWBERRIES REBECCA

2 qts. fresh strawberries,	1 cup light brown sugar,	1 Tbsp. cinnamon
washed & stemmed	firmly packed	Fresh mint for garnish
2 cups sour cream	1 Tbsp. vanilla	

Place berries in large bowl. Combine next 4 ingredients; pour over berries; garnish with mint. May make sauce ahead, and refrigerate. That Easy! Impressive!
Serves 8.

David Wallace, MY PERSONAL CHEF, Tyler, Texas

REAL TEXAS FOLK'S FACT:
Real Texas Folk are so proud of Texas they can't sleep at night! In fact when they do sleep they dream about Texas because inside every Texan's brain is a photograph of the map of Texas — there's one in his heart too!

GREAT FLAVORS' VERY BEST LEMON BARS

1/3 cup butter, melted
1/3 cup brown sugar, packed
1 cup flour
Pinch of salt

1/2 cup pecans, chopped
1/4 cup sugar
1 (8 oz.) pkg. cream cheese
1 egg

2 Tbsps. milk
1 Tbsp. fresh lemon juice
1 tsp. vanilla

Cream butter and sugar; add next 3 ingredients; mix well until crumbly; take out 1 cup mixture; pat the rest into lightly greased 8-inch square pan; bake 10 minutes at 350°. Combine rest of ingredients; beat well; spread over crust; top with 1 cup reserved mixture; bake at 325° for 25 minutes. Excellent!
Yields 12 bars. (Easily doubled — Bake in 9x13-inch pan.)

MARY LOU'S BROWN SUGAR CUPCAKES

1/2 cup shortening
1 cup dark brown sugar,
  packed

2 eggs, well beaten
1 Tbsp. vanilla
Pinch of salt

1 cup flour
1/2 cup nuts, chopped

Cream shortening and sugar; mix in eggs and vanilla; stir in rest of ingredients. Fill **muffin** tins, lined with paper cups, two-thirds full; bake 20-30 minutes or until cake tester comes out clean. Wait a day to serve as they are even better the next day! Great for Picnics!!
Makes about 12 cupcakes.

Mary Lou Palmros, Graford, Texas

MARVELOUS PRALINE BROWNIES

2 (14 oz.) cans condensed
  milk

1 lb. box graham cracker
  crumbs

12 oz. pkg. semi-sweet
  chocolate chips

Mix well all ingredients. With wet hands, pat mixture into 9x13-inch pan; bake at 350° for 25 minutes. Cool; cut into 2-inch squares. Great! So Easy!!
Yields 24 squares.

Lee Kennedy, Mesquite, Texas

OLD FASHIONED SUGAR TEA CAKES

1 cup vegetable oil	1 tsp. vanilla	1 tsp. soda
1 cup butter	2 eggs, beaten	Vegetable oil
1 cup sugar	4 cups flour	Sugar for dipping
1 cup powdered sugar	1 tsp. salt	

Cream first 5 ingredients; add eggs; stir in flour, salt, and soda; mix well; chill dough. Roll dough into small balls. Coat bottom of smooth glass plate with oil; dip each ball in sugar; press against oiled plate to flatten; repeat process with each cookie; bake 10 minutes at 350°. Cool on wire rack.

Makes 6 dozen.

"These wonderful cookies are served every day at the Mall's TEA ROOM!"

Chef David Wallace, TYLER SQUARE ANTIQUE MALL

BUNUELOS
(Christmas Fritters)

1 tsp. cinnamon	1 tsp. baking powder	½ cup warm water
½ cup sugar	1 Tbsp. shortening	Vegetable oil
2 cups flour	1 egg	

Mix cinnamon and sugar. Separately, mix well next 4 ingredients. Add water; knead until dough is smooth, about 5 minutes; shape into 24 balls; cover; let stand 30 minutes at room temperature. Roll balls out with rolling pin; be sure each strip is about ¼-inch thick. Place dough strips on large cloth about ½-inch apart; let rest 10 minutes; stretch dough with hands making sure not to tear. Fry in hot oil (375°), 3-4 inches deep, until golden brown on each side. Remove; sprinkle each side with cinnamon mixture. Very Delicious!!

Makes 2 dozen.   Victoria Guevara, Farmers Branch, Texas

TEXAS FACT:
Farmers Branch, founded in the mid 1800's in Dallas county, had the very first church, school, and blacksmith shop in the county, and today more than 60 Fortune 500 companies have offices in Farmers Branch!

SOUTH OF THE BORDER TREASURES

1 cup flour
¾ cup brown sugar
Pinch of salt
1 cup quick oats
½ tsp. baking soda
1½ sticks butter, melted
1 (6 oz.) pkg. chocolate chips
¾ cup pecans, chopped
¾ cup caramel ice cream
  topping
3 Tbsps. flour

With electric mixer, combine first 6 ingredients; press ½ crust into 9-inch square pan; bake at 350° for 10 minutes; remove; cover with chips and nuts. Mix topping with flour; spread over chips and nuts; top with rest of crust mixture; bake 15-20 minutes more or until golden; chill 2 hours. Serve cut in squares. Treasures Indeed!
Makes about 3 dozen.

CHRISTMAS SUGAR COOKIES

2 cups shortening
2¼ cups sugar
1 Tbsp. vanilla
3 eggs
4 Tbsps. milk
6 cups flour
4½ tsps. baking powder
¾ tsp. salt
4 Tbsps. butter
2 cups powdered sugar
2 tsps. vanilla

With mixer, cream first 3 ingredients; add eggs; beat until fluffy; add milk. Sift next 3 ingredients together; add to creamed mixture; divide dough into fourths; wrap in plastic wrap; chill 1 hour; roll out on waxed paper (if too stiff, add a little milk). Cut with cookie cutter; bake 6-8 minutes at 350°; cool. To make icing, mix well rest of ingredients. Spread on cookies.
Makes about 9 dozen.

Mignon Marsh, Tyler, Texas

DALLAS WALNUT WAFERS

1 stick butter
1 cup sugar
2 eggs
1 tsp. vanilla
½ tsp. salt
1 tsp. baking soda
2 Tbsps. flour
1½ cups walnuts, chopped

Cream butter and sugar; add next 3 ingredients. Combine soda and flour; fold into batter; fold in nuts. Cover cookie sheet with foil; drop batter onto foil, by teaspoonfuls, 3-inches apart. Bake 8-10 minutes at 350° or until brown around edges; cool.
Makes 40 marvelous cookies!

Nancy Lemmon, Dallas, Texas

BUTTERSCOTCH MERINGUE COOKIES

2 egg whites, beaten until stiff   *1 tsp. vanilla*   *8 ozs. butterscotch chips*
⅔ cup sugar   *1 cup nuts, chopped*

Preheat oven to 350°. To whites, add sugar; beat; fold in remaining ingredients. Cover cookie sheet with aluminum foil; drop batter by spoonfuls onto cookie sheet; put in oven; turn off heat; leave overnight. Cookies will be done that morning!
Makes 6 dozen delicious cookies! (Easily doubled)

Dottie Peek, Austin, Texas

LITTLE BITS OF HEAVEN

1 cup peanut butter   *2 eggs*   *1 tsp. cinnamon*
1 stick butter   *1 cup flour*   *1 (16 oz.) bag Hershey's Kisses*
1 cup brown sugar, packed   *1 tsp. baking powder*   *Powdered sugar*

Cream first 3 ingredients; beat in eggs. Combine 3 dry ingredients; add, slowly, to creamed mixture. Chill dough 30 minutes or more, overnight if possible. Measure dough in level teaspoons; put on cookie sheet; press 1 kiss in cookie's center; bake at 350° 10-12 minutes; cool slightly; roll in sugar.
Makes 4-5 dozen.

Marti Turner, Houston, Texas

TEXAS PECAN CHOCOLATE COOKIES

1 (14 oz.) can condensed milk   *1 (12 oz.) pkg. semi-sweet*   *1 cup plus 2 Tbsps. flour*
6 Tbsps. butter   *chocolate chips*   *36-48 pecan halves*

In saucepan over medium heat, mix well first 3 ingredients; stir until chocolate melts; remove from heat. Add flour; stir until blended; cool 10 minutes. Roll dough into large marble sized balls; place on ungreased cookie sheet; press a pecan half in center of each. Bake at 300° for 6-8 minutes until cookies are firm on outside but soft inside. Cookies Will Quickly Disappear!
Makes 3-4 dozen. (Easily doubled)

Sherry Ferguson, GREAT FLAVORS OF TEXAS

NUTMEG BUTTER COOKIES

2 sticks butter	*1⅓ cups pecans, chopped*	*½ cup powdered sugar*
½ cup sugar	*2 cups flour, sifted*	*2 tsps. nutmeg*
1 tsp. vanilla		

Cream butter and sugar until fluffy; stir in vanilla and nuts. Gradually, add flour; mix well; chill dough 30 minutes. Shape into 1-inch balls; bake at 325° on lightly greased cookie sheet for 25-30 minutes or until light golden brown. Combine sugar and nutmeg; roll warm cookies in mixture. *Makes 4 dozen.*

"These are our family's favorites at Christmas!"

Mary Denny, San Antonio, Texas

WINNER CHOCOLATE PEANUT BUTTER COOKIES

1 cup peanut butter	*1 stick butter*	*Scant ¼ cup paraffin*
1½ cups powdered sugar	*16 ozs. chocolate chips*	*(chipped)*

Cream first 3 ingredients; refrigerate 1-2 hours. Roll dough into small (marble-sized) balls; put on cookie sheets; refrigerate. In top of double boiler, melt rest of ingredients. Take cookies, one at a time; dip, using a toothpick, each into chocolate mixture; put cookie on waxed paper to dry; chill until firm. Cookies keep in refrigerator. Freeze well. *Makes 6 dozen.*

"These cookies are nice to add to an assortment of tea cookies at receptions and are a real winner with guests!"

Genie Calgaard, San Antonio, Texas

TEXAS GRAHAMS

2 sticks butter, melted	*½ cup pecans, chopped*	*24 graham crackers*
1 cup brown sugar, packed		

Boil butter and sugar for 2 minutes; add nuts; spread over crackers; place crackers on jelly roll pan; bake 10 minutes at 350°; cool slightly; separate. Easy, Delicious, and Children Love!

Nell Phillips, Beaumont, Texas

HATTIE HASIE'S PEANUT BRITTLE

Butter for pans   *3 Tbsps. water*   *2 cups raw peanuts*
3 cups sugar   *Pinch of salt*   *2 tsps. baking soda*
1 cup white corn syrup

Butter 2 large baking pans. In saucepan over medium heat, cook next 4 ingredients until thread forms when dropped (238° on candy thermometer) from a spoon. (Mixture will foam up in cooking.) Add nuts; cook until golden brown; add soda; stir quickly; put into pans; cool; break into pieces.
Makes about 2 pounds.

Hattie Hasie, Lubbock, Texas

Hattie is famous for her peanut brittle. She has shared her wonderful confection and bright spirit all over Texas for many years, sending boxes to family and friends!

MEXICAN CANDY

7 Tbsps. milk   *1 cup brown sugar*   *1 cup pecans, broken*
1 cup white sugar

In heavy saucepan, combine milk and sugars; cook until soft ball forms in cold water; add nuts; beat until mixed; drop by spoonfuls onto waxed paper. Wonderful!
Yields 2 dozen.

MILLION DOLLAR FUDGE

4½ cups sugar   *Pinch of salt*   *1 pt. marshmallow creme*
2 Tbsps. butter   *12 ozs. German chocolate bars*   *2 cup nuts, chopped*
12 ozs. evaporated milk   *12 ozs. semi-sweet chocolate chips*

In 3-quart saucepan; combine first 4 ingredients; bring to boil; stir constantly; boil 6 minutes. Separately, break up chocolate bars; add rest of ingredients; mix; add boiled mixture; stir until smooth; pour into buttered dish; refrigerate overnight; cut in pieces; store in airtight containers. Great!
Makes about 6 dozen.

Dottie Peek, Austin, Texas

TEXAS DELICIOUS CARAMELS

2 cups sugar
1 cup brown sugar, packed
1 cup light corn syrup
1 cup heavy cream
1 cup milk
2 sticks butter
1 1/4 tsps. vanilla

In saucepan, combine first 6 ingredients; cook over medium heat; stir occasionally to firm ball stage (248° on candy thermometer); remove from heat; add vanilla. Pour into buttered 8x8x2-inch pan; cool in refrigerator; cut into squares; store in tins in refrigerator. Enjoy!!
Makes 2 1/2 dozen.

Genie Calgaard, San Antonio, Texas

TEXAS RICH PECAN PRALINES

2 cups sugar
1 cup buttermilk
1 tsp. baking soda
Pinch of salt
2 Tbsps. butter
2 1/3 cups pecan halves

In heavy saucepan, combine first 4 ingredients over medium heat; cook 5 minutes or registers 210° on candy thermometer; stir frequently, scraping bottom and sides of pan; add butter and pecans; cook 5 minutes or candy forms soft ball in cold water (230° on candy thermometer); remove from heat; cool 15-20 minutes. Beat until creamy; drop by tablespoonfuls onto waxed paper; chill.
Makes 30 pralines.

Hattie Hasie, Lubbock, Texas

ABILENE TUMBLEWEEDS

12 oz. pkg. butterscotch chips
2 Tbsps. peanut butter
12 oz. can peanuts
4 oz. can shoestring potatoes

In top of double boiler, melt first 2 ingredients; add peanuts and potatoes; mix well; drop onto waxed paper; cool. That Easy! That Good!
Makes 2 dozen.

Sandra Broesche, Abilene, Texas

TEXAS FESTIVAL AND PLACE:
Poteet, the center of the truck-farming region in South Texas, is the Strawberry Capital of the World and produces 40% of Texas' strawberries annually. Poteet is home to the world's largest Strawberry Monument, a giant replica of a strawberry that is 7 feet tall and weighs 1,600 pounds!! The Strawberry Festival is held in Poteet the second weekend in April and features a parade, rodeo, carnival, and a strawberry contest!

LA VONA'S PEACH COBBLER

1 stick butter
1 cup Bisquick
1 cup sugar

⅔ cup milk
1 (28 oz.) can peaches or fresh peaches

½ cup sugar
Cinnamon

Melt butter in 9x13-inch pan. Mix next 3 ingredients; stir into butter in pan; spoon peaches and about ½-⅔ cup juice from can over batter. Sprinkle ½ cup sugar on top; cover heavily with cinnamon; bake 350° for 45-55 minutes. Super Warm with Ice Cream!

Serves 4-6.

Linda Sue Barnes, George West, Texas

WAXAHACHIE APPLE PIE

5 medium apples, peeled, pared, & sliced
1 cup sugar
¼ cup flour

Dash of salt
½ tsp. cinnamon
½ tsp. nutmeg
½ cup butter

1 9-inch whole wheat pie crust
1 whole wheat pie crust, cut in strips

Place apples in unbaked crust; combine sugar and next 5 ingredients; pour over apples; place strips on top to form a lattice. Bake at 300° for 1¼ hours. Excellent!

WONDERFUL WHOLE WHEAT PIE CRUST

1 cup whole wheat flour
1 cup all purpose flour

1 tsp. salt
⅔ cup shortening

½ cup cold water

Combine flours and salt; cut in shortening until mixture looks like small granules; add water; mix until dough forms a ball. Divide in half; wrap in plastic wrap; refrigerate. Use half for crust and other half for lattice; roll out on waxed paper; cover; refrigerate again before using.

Makes 2 pie crusts.

Ed Ford, Waxahachie, Texas

TEXAS PLACE AND FESTIVAL:
Waxahachie, located in East Texas, is noted for an abundance of Victorian-style homes, elaborate with "gingerbread" trim. Waxahachie hosts Scarborough Faire each spring for eight weekends (mid April-June). This springtime Renaissance fair features arts, crafts, foods, and medieval entertainment for one and all!

SUPER DELICIOUS CARAMEL PIE

2 cups sugar, divided equally
2 cups milk
¼ cup flour
3 Tbsps. butter

6 egg yolks, beaten
2 tsps. vanilla
1 9-inch pie shell, baked & cooled

6 egg whites, beaten stiff with 5 Tbsps. sugar

In skillet over low heat, brown 1 cup sugar; add milk; simmer until sugar dissolves. Separately, combine 1 cup sugar, flour, and next 3 ingredients; add hot "milk sugar;" stir; return mixture to skillet; cook until thick. Pour into pie shell; cool; spread whites over filling to edges of crust; bake at 350° for 12-15 minutes or until meringue is golden. Special!

Marcella Henderson, Denton, Texas

When Marcella was 8 years old, she learned how to make this pie from a neighbor. She, now, has been making this superb pie for over 80 years!!

CHOCOLATE ALMOND BAR PIE

9 (1.45 oz.) chocolate bars with almonds

1 (8 oz.) container Cool Whip
1 9-inch chocolate cookie crust

1 cup heavy cream, whipped

Melt candy; mix with topping; pour into pie crust; refrigerate. To serve, top with whipped cream. As Impressive as it is Easy to Make!!

Janie Means, Dallas, Texas

TEXAS BIG:
Denton, Texas, is home to Texas Woman's University (TWU) which is the largest university for women in the United States!

TEXAS FACT AND PLACE:
Houston, the fourth largest city in the United States, is one of the nation's largest seaports. Houston's Astrodome is the world's first air conditioned, domed stadium for baseball and football. The Astrodome's size is such that an 18-story building would fit inside it!

EASY 'N DELICIOUS CHOCOLATE CHESS PIE

1 square German sweet
   chocolate
½ cup butter
¾ cup sugar

1 (7 oz.) can evaporated milk
3 eggs, beaten
¼ tsp. salt
1 tsp. vanilla

1 9-inch pie crust, unbaked
1 cup heavy cream, whipped
   <u>or</u> vanilla <u>or</u> coffee ice
   cream

In saucepan over low heat, mix butter and chocolate; heat until melted; stir in next 5 ingredients; pour into pie shell. Bake at 350° for 30 minutes or until center puffs up and is fairly firm; cool. Serve topped with whipped or ice cream. The coffee ice cream is wonderful with this pie!!

Martha Lou Rugeley, Wichita Falls, Texas

THE "FUDGIEST" PIE

2 cups sugar
½ cup flour
4 eggs, beaten

2 tsps. vanilla
2 sticks butter
½ cup cocoa

1 9-inch pie crust, unbaked

Mix well first 4 ingredients. In saucepan, over low heat, melt butter with cocoa; add to egg mixture; mix well. Pour into pie crust; bake at 350° for 45 minutes; do not overbake. Cool before serving. Good!

Minnie Bladen, Dallas, Texas

Minnie has been cooking at Armstrong Elementary School in the Highland Park School District for 30 years! Former students come back on a regular basis for a taste of Minnie's great food!!

TEXAS FESTIVAL:
The Rattlesnake Roundup, held annually in Sweetwater, is one of West Texas most unusual and interesting events. Guided bus tours take everyone to view the snakes in their natural habitat! Other activities include a gun and coin show, flea market, dancing, and snake handling!

CORNMEAL CHESS PIE

3 eggs, beaten
2½ cups sugar
¼ cup heavy cream

1 stick butter, melted
½ cup cornmeal
1 tsp. vanilla

1 9-inch pie shell, unbaked

Mix well first 6 ingredients; pour mixture into pie shell. Bake at 350° for 50-60 minutes or until top is golden brown.

Faye Gilmore, Possom Kingdom Lake, Texas

PORT ARTHUR CHOCOLATE CHIP COOKIE PIES

2 sticks butter, melted
2 cups sugar
1 cup all purpose flour

4 eggs, well beaten
2 tsps. vanilla
18 ozs. chocolate morsels

2 cups pecans, chopped
2 9-inch pie crusts
Vanilla ice cream

Combine butter and sugar; add next 3 ingredients; mix well; stir in chocolate and nuts; pour ½ batter in each crust. Bake at 350° for 45-50 minutes or until firm in center. Serve warm topped with ice cream. So Good that Making Two Pies is a Necessity if the Cook wants Any!!

EVELYN'S STRAWBERRY PARFAIT PIE

1 (3.9 oz.) pkg. strawberry
    gelatin
1¼ cups water, boiling

1 pt. vanilla ice cream
1 (12 oz.) pkg. frozen
    strawberries, thawed

1 8-inch pie crust, baked
Whipped cream

Dissolve gelatin in water; add ice cream by spoonfuls; stir until melted; chill mixture until thickened, but not set, about 15-20 minutes. Fold in berries; pour in pie crust; chill until firm, at least 30 minutes. Serve topped with whipped cream. A Real Texas Treat!!

Susan Bagwell, Dallas, Texas

TEXAS BIG:
Port Arthur, Texas, located on the northwest shore of Lake Sabine which is the largest salt water lake in East Texas, is the site of the world's largest oil refining/petroleum complex! Oil cargo tonnage, which annually averages about 23,000,000, justifies Port Arthur's claim that "We Oil the World." Nearly a million barrels of oil are refined in the area daily!

GRANDMA SARA'S NO-FUSS PECAN PIE

1 cup white corn syrup
1 cup dark brown sugar
1/3 cup margarine, melted

1 cup pecans (heaping!)
2 whole eggs, beaten
1 tsp. vanilla

1/4 tsp. salt
1 9-inch pie crust, unbaked

Mix well first 7 ingredients; pour into pie shell; bake at 350° for 45-50 minutes or until set. Serve with whipped or ice cream. Super!

Charlotte Webberman, Dallas, Texas

OLD FASHIONED BROWN SUGAR PIE

2 cups brown sugar
3 eggs
1 stick butter, melted

1½ tsps. vanilla
1 9-inch pie shell, unbaked
1 cup heavy cream, whipped

Fresh strawberries or kiwi for garnish

Beat well sugar and eggs; add butter and vanilla; beat; pour in crust; bake at 350° for 30 minutes or until firm; cool. Serve topped with whipped cream and fresh fruit. Heavenly!!
Serves 6-8.

MARVELOUS PEANUT BUTTER PIE

3 ozs. cream cheese, room temperature
1 cup powdered sugar

8 ozs. Cool Whip, thawed
1/2 cup crunchy peanut butter, room temperature

1 9-inch chocolate pie crust
Chocolate shavings, pecans, or Reese's Pieces, optional

With mixer, beat cream cheese; mix in next 3 ingredients; pour into crust; chill. Pretty topped with chocolate, pecan pieces, or candy. Wonderful with graham cracker crust too! Quick, Easy and Good!

Rubye Dyer, Houston, Texas

TEXAS NOTABLE:
Tex Ritter, the famous country and western singer, called Nederland, Texas, home. Ritter's contributions to country music were recognized when he was named to the Country Music Hall of Fame. The song that he is most famous for is probably his recording of the title song from the Gary Cooper film, HIGH NOON. The Windmill Museum in Netherland features mementos from the singer's life.

DELICIOUS LITTLE PECAN TARTS

1 stick margarine
½ cup sugar
2 egg yolks
1 tsp. almond extract

2 cups flour, sifted
1 stick margarine
⅓ cup dark corn syrup

1 cup powdered sugar
1 cup pecans, chopped
48 pecan halves

TO MAKE TART SHELLS: In the order given, combine first 5 ingredients until ball of dough forms. Press evenly into ungreased tiny tart or miniature muffin tins; bake 8-10 minutes at 400°. **TO MAKE FILLING:** In saucepan, over high heat, combine stick margarine and next 2 ingredients; bring to boil; remove from heat; stir in nuts; pour into shells; top with pecan halves. Bake at 350° for 5 minutes. Outstanding!

Makes 48 miniature tarts.

Ann Willard, Dallas, Texas

SAWMILL PIE

1½ cups pecans, chopped
1½ cups graham cracker
   crumbs
1½ cups coconut

1½ cups sugar
1 (6 oz.) pkg. semi-sweet
   chocolate chips
7 egg whites, beaten stiff

1 9-inch pie crust, unbaked
Vanilla ice cream

Mix well first 6 ingredients; pour into pie crust. Bake at 350° for 35 minutes or until filling is firm. Serve warm and topped with ice cream. Wonderful and Very Easy!

Bobbie Bohall, Colleyville, Texas

TEXAS NOTABLE:
Lyndon B. Johnson, the Thirty-Sixth President of the United States, was born in Johnson City, Texas, in 1908. Johnson, the quintessential public servant, was a member of the nation's House of Representatives (1937-49), and Senate (1949-61), Vice President of the United States (1960-63), and President from 1963-1969. His career in Washington is unique because only a handful of Americans (including Jefferson and Adams) have served the nation at all levels of national (elected) office. As President, Johnson's domestic agenda was laudable and buoyant for it resulted in the passage of much necessary and important legislation which included the Civil Rights Act of 1964 and the Voting Rights Act of 1968. In 1969 after serving his country for 36 years, the President returned to his beloved Texas with his wife, Lady Bird.

PERFECTION ICE CREAM PIE
(With Peanut Brittle Crust)

2/3 cup graham cracker crumbs, finely crushed
1/4 cup peanut brittle (page 169), finely crushed
2 Tbsps. sugar
2 Tbsps. butter, softened

1 qt. vanilla ice cream, softened
6 egg whites
1/4 tsp. cream of tartar
1/4 tsp. vanilla
Pinch of salt

6 Tbsps. sugar
1 stick butter
1 cup sugar
2 ozs. unsweetened chocolate
1 (5 oz.) can evaporated milk
1 tsp. vanilla

TO MAKE CRUST: Mix well first 4 ingredients; press into a 9-inch pie pan; bake at 350° for 3 minutes; cool. TO MAKE FILLING: Fill cooled crust with ice cream; smooth top with spatula; freeze to hard. In large bowl, beat egg whites to foamy; add next 3 ingredients; beat; add sugar, 1 tablespoon at a time; beat until stiff peaks form. Preheat oven to broiling; top ice cream with meringue, sealed to edges of crust; brown under broiler 1-2 minutes; watch carefully; refreeze. TO MAKE FUDGE SAUCE: Over medium heat, melt butter and next 2 ingredients; stir in milk and vanilla; stir constantly until thickened; refrigerate until ready to use. Reheat before serving; top each pie slice with sauce. Excellent!

Deanna Brown, Dallas, Texas

ELIZABETH'S BEST PUMPKIN PIE

1 (1lb. 13 oz.) can pumpkin
1 cup light brown sugar
1 cup white sugar
2 Tbsps. molasses
1/4 tsp. powdered cloves

3 tsps. cinnamon
3 tsps. ginger
1 tsp. salt
4 eggs, slightly beaten

1 (12 oz.) can Carnation evaporated milk plus 4 ozs. water
2 9-inch deep dish pie crusts

With electric mixer, combine first 10 ingredients in the order given; pour into crusts; bake at 500° for 10 minutes; lower heat to 300°; bake 1 hour or until filling is set.

"The pie is yummy topped with whipped cream and is the best pumpkin pie in the whole world!"

Elizabeth Findling, San Antonio, Texas

SOUTHERN APPLE CUSTARD PIE

1 cup applesauce
1 cup sugar
3 Tbsps. fresh lemon juice
4 eggs, beaten

2 Tbsps. butter, melted
Pinch of salt
½ tsp. nutmeg
½ tsp. cinnamon

1 9-inch pie crust
Brown sugar

Mix well first 8 ingredients; pour in unbaked pie crust; bake at 350° for an hour or until filling is set; sprinkle brown sugar over warm pie. Good! A Different Custard Pie!

DEATH BY CHOCOLATE PIE SUPREME

1 stick Betty Crocker pie crust mix
¼ cup light brown sugar, packed
1 Tbsp. cold water
1 Tbsp. vanilla
1¼ cups walnuts, chopped & toasted

6 ozs. Hershey chocolate chips
2 egg whites
¼ cup light brown sugar, packed
½ pt. heavy cream
8 ozs. cream cheese

½ cup light brown sugar, packed
⅛ tsp. salt
½ pt. heavy cream, whipped
4 (1.55 oz.) Hershey Milk Chocolate Bars, grated

To make crust, mix well first 4 ingredients; add nuts; press into bottom and sides of 9-inch round metal pie pan. Bake 15 minutes at 375°; cool. To make filling, lightly grease top of double boiler; put chips in top; melt; cool. Separately, beat egg whites until soft peaks form; add ¼-cup sugar; beat until stiff peaks form. Separately, whip cream until holds peaks. Separately, with electric mixer, blend cream cheese and next 3 ingredients; add cooled chocolate; mix until smooth. Fold whipped cream into egg whites; fold gently into cream cheese mixture; pour into cooled crust; refrigerate overnight. To serve, generously top each slice of pie with whipped cream; sprinkle with grated chocolate.

"My mother perfected this dream dessert, which collected a grand prize at a local 'Death By Chocolate' party attended by avid chocoholics!!"

Ellen Tipton, Houston, Texas

TEXAS LAGNIAPPE
(A Little Something Extra)

LADY BIRD JOHNSON'S PEDERNALES RIVER CHILI

4 lbs. chili meat (round *or* chuck steak, very coarsely ground)

1 large onion, chopped

2-5 cloves garlic *or* to taste

1 tsp. ground oregano

1 tsp. cumin

6 tsps. commercial chili powder

1½ cups canned whole tomatoes

2 generous dashes liquid hot sauce

Salt & pepper to taste

2 cups hot water *or* canned beef stock (*or* 1 cup hot water *or* stock plus 1 can beer)

1 Tbsp. masa harina *or* to taste, optional

In heavy frying pan or Dutch oven, cook meat, onion, and garlic until light colored. Add rest of ingredients; bring to boil; lower heat; simmer at least an hour. Skim off fat during cooking. If desired, thicken with masa harina by sprinkling over top of chili; then, stir it into chili throughout. *Serves 8-10.*

"Real Texas chili does not have beans in it, but if you must add beans, make them home cooked pinto beans, well drained!!"

Mrs. Lyndon Baines Johnson, Austin & Johnson City, Texas

Lady Bird Johnson is a Texas Notable in her own right (see TEXAS NOTABLE, page 14) as is her husband, Lyndon (see TEXAS NOTABLE, page 176)!

TEXAS BIG:
The largest livestock auction in the world is in Amarillo!

TEXAS TREASURE:
Mary Martin, a native of Weatherford, Texas, has had a distinguished career on the Broadway stage and in motion pictures. Perhaps her most famous role was that of Peter Pan on Broadway and later on television. Weatherford has honored Miss Martin by dedicating a statue of Peter Pan (located there) to her! Mary Martin is the real-life mother of the actor, Larry Hagman, who played the infamous J.R. Ewing on the television series DALLAS.

COMPANY BEEF TENDERS

1 lb. beef tender, trimmed & tied   *Salt & pepper to taste*

About 2-3 hours before serving, preheat oven to 450°. Place meat on baking dish; cook at 450° for 35 minutes. While tender is cooking, cut 2 large sheets of aluminum foil in which to wrap cooked tenders. Then, line a small styrofoam cooler with newspapers. When tender is done, quickly wrap securely in foil; place in cooler on top of newspapers; cover with more newspapers to further insulate; cover all with top of cooler. <u>Do not open until time to serve</u>! To serve, salt and pepper tender; slice. Meat will be warm and medium rare. Wonderful!
Serves 8.

"You may serve this totally Texas entree with your favorite sauce or just the way it is! This is a perfect recipe to use when entertaining because it allows you to be with your guests instead of in the kitchen!!

Camille Warmington, Houston, Texas

SAVORY BEEF 'N BEANS

1 onion, chopped	*Salt & pepper to taste*	*1 (1 lb.) can kidney beans*
1 green pepper, chopped	*1 Tbsp. flour*	*1/4-1/2 lb. round steak,*
1/4 cup salad oil	*1/2 tsp. sugar*	*chopped, <u>not</u> ground*
1 (10 oz.) can tomato soup	*1/4 cup Cheddar cheese*	*1/4 cup water, hot*

In skillet, brown onion and pepper in oil; add soup and seasonings; cook 5 minutes; add next 3 ingredients; mix; add beans. Separately, brown meat slightly in a little oil. Stir in water; add to bean mixture. Bake at 275° for an hour. The more beef you add the heartier the dish! Without the beef, the beans are excellent with barbecue or a picnic-style meal!!
Serves 4-6.

"These savory beans always get raves!"

Evelyn Bennett, Austin, Texas

CHAMPION OF CHAMPIONS REUNION PEA CASSEROLE

1 lb. regular pork sausage, fried, drained, & crumbled
2 cups black-eyed peas, cooked & coarsely mashed
1 (4 oz.) can chopped green chilies
1 tsp. garlic powder
1/4 tsp. cumin
1/4 tsp. oregano
1/2 tsp. salt
1/2 tsp. pepper
4 Tbsps. margarine
2 cups yellow squash, sliced in 1/4-inch rounds
1 cup onion, chopped
4 eggs, well beaten
2 cups Mozzarella cheese, shredded
2 cups Cheddar cheese, shredded
2 pkgs. crescent style rolls
1/2-1 cup bread crumbs, buttered

Combine first 8 ingredients; mix thoroughly; set aside. In large skillet over low heat, melt margarine; add squash and onion; saute until tender. Remove from heat; cool 5 minutes. Separately combine eggs and cheeses together; fold into squash. Make roll dough into 2 long rectangles; place in lightly greased 9x13-inch pan; press dough over bottom and up sides to form a crust. Layer sausage/pea mixture on bottom of crust; top with squash mixture; sprinkle with bread crumbs. Bake at 350° for 25-30 minutes; let "set" for 15 minutes before serving.
Serves 8-10.   Joyce Carroll, Athens, Texas

DIANE'S GRAND CHAMPION "PEA-TATOES" APPETIZERS

18-20 small new potatoes
1 oz. cream cheese
1 cup Cheddar cheese, shredded
2 cups black-eyed peas, drained
6 slices bacon, cooked, crumbled, & 1 Tbsp. drippings reserved
1/4 cup green onion, thinly sliced
Garlic salt & pepper to taste

Bake potatoes in covered dish at 350° for 45 minutes or until done; cool. Slice off tops; scoop out centers. With potato masher, mix potato pulp, cream cheese, and 1/2 cup Cheddar cheese. Add peas and bacon; mix well. Separately, saute onions with reserved bacon drippings; add to pea mixture; season. Stuff potato shells; sprinkle with remaining 1/2 cup cheese; heat at 350° until hot and cheese has melted, about 10-15 minutes. Super!
Makes 18-20.   Diane Milner, Murchison, Texas

Both Joyce's and Diane's recipes were first place winners at the Black-Eyed Pea Jamboree!!

WONDERFUL CURRIED DEVILED EGGS
(With Shrimp Sauce)

8 hard-boiled eggs, sliced
   lengthwise
1/2 stick butter, melted
1/4 tsp. salt
Dash of pepper

1/4 tsp. prepared mustard
1 tsp. minced onion
1/4 tsp. curry powder
2 Tbsps. butter
2 Tbsps. flour

1 cup milk
1 (10³/4 oz.) can shrimp soup
1/2 cup Cheddar cheese, grated
1 cup bread crumbs, buttered

Remove yolks; place in bowl; mix with next 6 ingredients. Mash filling; mix thoroughly. Spoon filling into egg whites; place in baking dish yellow side up. To make sauce, in saucepan over medium heat, melt 2 tablespoons butter, stir in flour, and cook 1-2 minutes. Slowly add milk; stir, and cook until thick. Stir in soup and cheese; cook until cheese melts. Pour sauce over eggs; sprinkle with crumbs; bake at 350° for 30 minutes. A Wonderful Party Dish!
Serves 8. (Easily doubled)

Shirley Fancher, Amarillo, Texas

DELICIOUS BLACK-EYED PEA 'N CORNBREAD SALAD

2 pkgs. cornbread mix, baked
   per pkgs.' directions
8 slices bacon, cooked crisp &
   crumbled

1½ bunches green onions,
   chopped
1 cup mayonnaise
1 cup black-eyed peas

4 hard-boiled eggs, chopped
1 bell pepper, chopped
2 large tomatoes, chopped

Crumble cornbread into large bowl; add remaining ingredients. Mix well. Refrigerate until ready to serve. Marvelous and Easy!
Serves 8-10.

Bonnie Conner, Athens, Texas

TEXAS FESTIVAL:
Athens, Texas, is home to the Black-Eyed Pea Jamboree, which is held annually the third weekend in July. This unique festival pays homage to the South's favorite food and is appropriately held in Athens, the Black-Eyed Pea Capital of the World!! The festival features a parade, carnival, the "Miss Black-Eyed Pea" Beauty Pageant, a Pea Picker's Square Dance, and the Main Event — the Black-Eyed Pea Cook-off!!

CAPELLINI D'ANGELO WITH FRESH TOMATOES AND BASIL

1 lb. Angel Hair pasta
1/3 cup extra virgin olive oil
3 cloves garlic, minced
1/4 cup rich chicken stock

8 Roma tomatoes, peeled,
   seeded, & chopped
1/4 cup fresh basil, loosely
   packed & minced

3 Tbsps. fresh lemon juice
Salt & pepper to taste
1 cup Parmesan cheese,
   grated

Cook pasta in boiling water for 4-5 minutes; drain. Heat oil over medium heat; cook garlic; do <u>not</u> brown. Add pasta; toss well to coat; add next 3 ingredients. Toss to coat well. Season with lemon juice, salt and pepper. Serve topped with cheese. A Delicious Light Meal!!
Serves 4.

Chef Steve Valenti, PATRIZIO'S RESTAURANT, Dallas, Texas

GREAT FLAVORS' CHRISTMAS CASSEROLE FOR EIGHT

1 stick butter, melted
8 ozs. fresh mushrooms
1 (14 oz.) can artichoke
   hearts, drained
1 (16 oz.) carton sour cream

1 (8 oz.) can water chestnuts,
   drained
1 (8 oz.) can bamboo shoots,
   drained
Salt & pepper to taste

Dash of Worcestershire sauce
1-1½ cups Ritz cracker crumbs
¼-½ stick butter
Fresh parsley & pimento for
   garnish

Saute mushrooms (canned are okay) in butter; line bottom of 2-quart casserole with artichokes; scoop mushrooms out of butter; sprinkle over artichokes. In pan with butter, add sour cream; mix well; add next 4 ingredients; let simmer 4 minutes to blend flavors; pour over artichokes/mushrooms. Top with crumbs; dot with butter; bake at 350° until top is slightly browned and butter is melted. Garnish; serve warm; scoop to bottom for each serving to include artichokes!

"The parsley and pimentos provide festive Christmas colors! I use parsley and thick lemon slices for color when serving at non-holiday times. I developed the recipe while helping to prepare our family's 1979 Christmas dinner at my brother's home in Houston. In 1980, the recipe won first place in the SAN ANTONIO NEWS EXPRESS' COOKING CONTEST!"

Jan Bennett Steger, GREAT FLAVORS OF TEXAS

MOTHER'S BEST FRENCH TOAST

½ cup flour
1 tsp. baking powder
Dash of salt

½ cup milk
1 egg
5 slices white bread

2 tsps. cinnamon mixed with
3-4 Tbsps. powdered sugar
Hot oil for frying

Combine first 3 ingredients. Separately, mix well milk and egg. Add to dry ingredients. Cut each bread slice diagonally (do not remove crust). Dip bread in egg batter. Fry in hot oil until brown and puffy. Serve sprinkled with cinnamon mixture.
Serves 3-4. (Easily doubled)

"This French toast is a favorite of all mother's grandchildren!!"

Sue Phillips Philp, Beaumont, Texas

COLLIN STREET BAKERY CHOCOLATE CLUSTER COOKIES

2¾ cups sugar
3 Tbsps. bread flour
½ tsp. cream of tartar
1½ squares bitter chocolate

½ square semi-sweet
  chocolate
6 large egg whites
2 tsps. shortening

1½ tsps. vanilla
2½ cups pecan pieces
Waxed paper & Pam

In large saucepan, combine first 3 ingredients; add next 4 ingredients; place pan in pan of water over medium heat. Heat until chocolate melts and sugar dissolves; stir often. Remove from heat; add vanilla and nuts; mix well. Line cookie sheets with waxed paper; spray paper with Pam; drop batter by teaspoonfuls onto paper. Bake at 365° for 15-20 minutes. Do <u>not</u> overcook; cookies are done when soft in center. Wonderful!
Yields 4 dozen 2½-inch cookies!!

COLLIN STREET BAKERY, Corsicana, Texas

TEXAS FACTS AND PLACE:
Corsicana, located in East Texas, had one of Texas' first oil refineries, built in 1897, and was the first city in Texas to use natural gas for fuel and lighting. Corsicana is the home of the Collin Street Bakery which since 1896 has produced the world's most famous deluxe fruitcake! These delicious cakes are shipped each year to every state in the United States and to 100 foreign countries!

GOVERNOR'S MANSION CHOCOLATE MOUSSE

12 ozs. semi-sweet chocolate
    morsels
3/4 cup espresso coffee
4 egg yolks

2 cups very cold heavy cream
1/4 cup sugar
Pinch of salt
8 egg whites

1/2 tsp. vanilla
Fresh mint sprigs

In saucepan, melt chocolate; stir constantly. Add espresso; cool mixture to room temperature. To cooled mixture, add egg yolks, one at a time, beating thoroughly after each addition. Whip 1 cup cream until thickened; gradually, add sugar, beating until cream is stiff. Beat egg whites with salt until stiff peaks form; gently fold whites into whipped cream. Stir 1/3 of cream mixture into chocolate mixture. Add remaining cream mixture; gently fold into chocolate. Pour mousse into 8 dessert cups or serving bowl; refrigerate 2 hours. At serving time, whip remaining 1 cup cream until thickened; add vanilla and whip to soft peaks. Top each serving of mousse with dollop of whipped cream; garnish with mint sprigs. Easy, Elegant, and Delicious!!
Serves 8.

Governor Ann W. Richards, Currently Serving as Texas' Forty-fifth Governor

Governor Richards' election to the highest office in the State of Texas is the culmination of a lifetime of public service — as a teacher, civil rights activist, Travis County Commissioner, and State Treasurer. She is committed to seeing that in Texas the people come first!

TEXAS FACT:
Texas' climate is as varied as its terrain. Amarillo, located in North Texas, averages 14 inches of snowfall per year while Brownsville, located in South Texas, has never had one snowflake fall!

Index

GREAT FLAVORS SERIES OF COOKBOOKS
Post Office Box 922
Pine Bluff, Arkansas 71613

_____ copies of GREAT FLAVORS OF TEXAS at $11.50 each _____
_____ copies of GREAT FLAVORS OF LOUISIANA at $9.50 each _____
_____ copies of GREAT FLAVORS OF MISSISSIPPI at $9.50 each _____
_____ copies of GREAT FLAVORS OF ARKANSAS at $9.50 each _____
_____ copies of MORE GREAT FLAVORS OF ARKANSAS at $9.50 each _____
TOTAL _____

EACH PER COPY PRICE INCLUDES POSTAGE, HANDLING, AND TAX.

TELEPHONE YOUR ORDER BY CALLING OUR 24-HOUR ANSWERING SERVICE
AT 501-536-8221 OR 1-800-874-5725.

ENCLOSED IS MY CHECK OR MONEY ORDER FOR $_____.
(FOR MASTER CARD OR VISA CHARGES, SEE PAGE 192.)

Name _____

Street _____

City_____ State _____ Zip _____

Charge to my: ☐  ☐

Account Number:

☐☐☐☐☐☐☐☐☐☐☐☐☐☐☐   ☐☐☐☐

Expiration Date: _____

Customer's Signature: _____

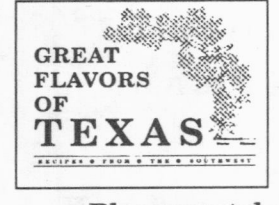   

Please watch for other Southern Flavors Publications and Products!!

Names and addresses of bookstores, gift shops, etc., in your area would be appreciated.

_____

_____

_____

_____